Kṛṣṇa Consciousness

THE MATCHLESS GIFT

BOOKS
by His Divine Grace
A.C. Bhaktivedanta Swami Prabhupāda

Bhagavad-gītā As It Is
Śrīmad-Bhāgavatam, Cantos 1-4 (13 Vols.)
Śrī Caitanya-caritāmṛta (3 Vols.)
Teachings of Lord Caitanya
The Nectar of Devotion
Śrī Īśopaniṣad
Easy Journey to Other Planets
Kṛṣṇa Consciousness: The Topmost Yoga System
Kṛṣṇa, The Supreme Personality of Godhead (2 Vols.)
Transcendental Teachings of Prahlād Mahārāja
Transcendental Teachings of Caitanya Mahāprabhu
Kṛṣṇa, the Reservoir of Pleasure
The Perfection of Yoga
Beyond Birth and Death
On the Way to Kṛṣṇa
Rāja-vidyā: The King of Knowledge
Elevation to Kṛṣṇa Consciousness
Lord Caitanya in Five Features
Back to Godhead Magazine (Founder)

A complete catalogue is available upon request.

International Society for Krishna Consciousness
3959 Landmark Street
Culver City, California 90230

ALL GLORY TO ŚRĪ GURU AND GAURĀṄGA

Kṛṣṇa Consciousness

THE MATCHLESS GIFT

by His Divine Grace
A.C. Bhaktivedanta Swami Prabhupāda

Founder-Ācārya
International Society for Krishna Consciousness

THE BHAKTIVEDANTA BOOK TRUST

New York · Los Angeles · London · Bombay

Readers interested in the subject matter
of this book are invited by
the International Society for Krishna Consciousness
to correspond with its Secretary.

International Society for Krishna Consciousness
3959 Landmark Street
Culver City, California 90230

First Printing, 1974: 25,000 copies

Library of Congress Catalog Card Number: 73-76634
International Standard Book Number: 0-912776-61-7

Printed in the United States of America.

1/Spiritual Knowledge Through Kṛṣṇa

The aim of this Kṛṣṇa consciousness movement is to bring all living entities back to their original consciousness. All living entities within the material world are, to varying degrees, afflicted with a type of madness. This Kṛṣṇa consciousness movement aims at curing man of his material disease and reestablishing his original consciousness. In a Bengali poem a great Vaiṣṇava poet has written, "When a man is haunted by ghosts, he can only speak nonsense. Similarly, anyone who is under the influence of material nature should be considered haunted, and whatever he speaks should be considered nonsense." One may be considered a great philosopher or great scientist, but if he is haunted by the ghost of *māyā*, illusion, whatever he theorizes and whatever he speaks is more or less nonsensical. Today we are given the example of a psychiatrist who, when requested to examine a murderer, proclaimed that since all the patients with whom he had come in contact were more or less crazy, the court could excuse the murderer on those grounds if it so desired. The point is that in the material world it is very difficult to find a sane living entity. The prevailing atmosphere of insanity in this world is all caused by the infection of material consciousness.

The purpose of this Hare Kṛṣṇa movement is to bring man back to his original consciousness, which is Kṛṣṇa consciousness, clear consciousness. When water falls from the clouds, it is uncontaminated like distilled water, but as soon as it touches the ground it becomes muddy and discolored. Similarly, we are originally pure spirit soul, part and parcel of Kṛṣṇa, and therefore our original constitutional position is as pure as God's. In *Bhagavad-gītā* Śrī Kṛṣṇa says:

mamaivāṁśo jīva-loke
jīva-bhūtaḥ sanātanaḥ
manaḥ ṣaṣṭhānīndriyāṇi
prakṛti-sthāni karṣati

"The living entities in this conditional world are My fragmental parts, and they are eternal. But due to conditioned life, they are struggling very hard with the six senses, which include the mind." (Bg. 15.7)

Thus all living entities are part and parcel of Kṛṣṇa. By Kṛṣṇa it should always be remembered that we are speaking of God, Kṛṣṇa denoting the all-attractive Supreme Personality of Godhead. As a fragment of gold is qualitatively the same as a gold reservoir, so the minute particles of Kṛṣṇa's body are therefore qualitatively as good as Kṛṣṇa. The chemical composition of God's body and the eternal spiritual body of the living entity is the same—spiritual. Thus originally, in our uncontaminated condition, we possessed a form as good as God's, but just as rain falls to the ground, so we come in contact with this material world, which is manipulated by the external material energy of Kṛṣṇa.

When we speak of external energy or material nature, the question may be raised, "Whose energy? Whose nature?" Material energy or nature is not active independently. Such a concept is foolish. In *Bhagavad-gītā* it is clearly stated that material nature does not work independently. When a foolish man sees a machine he may think that it is working automatically, but actually it is not—there is a driver, someone in control, although we sometimes cannot see the controller behind the machine due to our defective vision. There are many electronic mechanisms which work very wonderfully, but behind these intricate systems there is a scientist who pushes the button. This is very simple to understand: since a machine is matter, it cannot work on its own accord but must work under spiritual direction. A tape recorder works, but it works according to the plans and under the direction of a living entity, a human being. The machine is complete, but unless it is manipulated by a spirit soul, it cannot work. Similarly, we should understand that this cosmic manifestation which we call nature is a great machine and that behind this machine there is God, Kṛṣṇa. This is also affirmed in *Bhagavad-gītā* where Kṛṣṇa says:

mayādhyakṣeṇa prakṛtiḥ
sūyate sa-carācaram
hetunānena kaunteya
jagad viparivartate

"This material nature is working under My direction, O son of Kuntī, producing all the moving and unmoving beings, and by its rule this manifestation is created and annihilated again and again." (Bg. 9.10)

There are two kinds of entities—the moving (such as human beings, animals and insects) and non-moving (such as trees and mountains). Kṛṣṇa says that material nature, which controls both kinds of entities, is acting under His direction. Thus behind everything there is a supreme controller. Modern civilization does not understand this due to lack of knowledge; it is the purpose of this Society for Kṛṣṇa Consciousness, therefore, to enlighten all people who have been maddened by the influence of the three modes of material nature. In other words, our aim is to awaken mankind to its normal condition.

There are many universities, especially in the United States, and many departments of knowledge, but they are not discussing these points. Where is the department for this knowledge that we find given by Śrī Kṛṣṇa in *Bhagavad-gītā*? When I spoke before students and some faculty members at the Massachusetts Institute of Technology, the first question raised was: "Where is the technological department which is investigating the difference between a dead man and a living man?" When a man dies, something is lost. Where is the technology to replace it? Why don't scientists try to solve this problem? Because this is a very difficult subject matter, they set it aside and busily engage in the technology of eating, sleeping, mating and defending. However, Vedic literatures inform us that this is animal technology. Animals are also trying their best to eat well, to have an enjoyable sex life, to sleep peacefully, and to defend themselves. What then is the difference between man's knowledge and animals' knowledge? The fact is that man's knowledge should be developed to explore that difference between a living man and a dead man, a living body and a dead body. That spiritual knowledge was imparted by Kṛṣṇa to Arjuna in the beginning of *Bhagavad-gītā*. Being a friend of Kṛṣṇa's, Arjuna was a very intelligent man, but his knowledge, as all men's, was limited. Kṛṣṇa spoke, however, of subject matters which were beyond Arjuna's finite knowledge. These subjects are called *adhokṣaja* because our direct perception by which we acquire material knowledge fails to approach them. For example, we have many powerful microscopes to see what we cannot see with our limited vision, but there is no microscope that can show us the soul within the body. Nevertheless, the soul is there.

Bhagavad-gītā informs us that in this body there is a proprietor. I am the proprietor, and others are the proprietors of their bodies. I say, "My hand," but not "I hand." Since it is "my hand," I am different from the hand, being its owner. Similarly, we speak of "My eye," "My leg," "My this," "My that." In the midst of all of these objects which belong to me, where am I? The search for the answer to this question is the process of meditation. In real meditation, we ask, "Where am I? What am I?" We cannot find the answers to these questions by any material effort, and because of this all the universities are setting these questions aside. They say, "It is too difficult a subject." Or they brush it aside: "It is irrelevant." Thus engineers direct their attention to creating and attempting to perfect the horseless carriage and wingless bird. Formerly, horses were drawing carriages and there was no air pollution, but now there are cars and rockets, and the scientists are very proud. "We have invented horseless carriages and wingless birds," they boast. Although they invent imitation wings for the airplane or rocket, they cannot invent a soulless body. When they are able to actually do this, they will deserve credit. But such an attempt would necessarily be frustrated, for we know that there is no machine that can work without a spirit soul behind it. Even the most complicated computers need trained men to handle them. Similarly, we should know that this great machine, which is known as the cosmic manifestation, is manipulated by a supreme spirit. That is Kṛṣṇa. Scientists are searching for the ultimate cause or the ultimate controller of this material universe and are postulating different theories and proposals, but the real means for knowledge is very easy and perfect: we need only hear from the perfect person, Kṛṣṇa. By accepting the knowledge imparted in *Bhagavad-gītā,* anyone can immediately know that this great cosmic machine, of which the earth is a part, is working so wonderfully because there is a driver behind it—Kṛṣṇa.

Our process of knowledge is very easy. Kṛṣṇa's instruction, *Bhagavad-gītā,* is the principal book of knowledge given by the *ādi-puruṣa* Himself, the Supreme Primeval Person, the Supreme Personality of Godhead. He is indeed the perfect person. It may be argued that although we have accepted Him as a perfect person, there are many others who do not. But one should not think that this acceptance is whimsical; He is accepted as the perfect person on the evidence of many authorities. We do not accept Kṛṣṇa as perfect simply on the basis of our whims or sentiments. No—Kṛṣṇa is accepted as God by many

Vedic authorities like Vyāsadeva, the author of all Vedic literatures. The treasurehouse of knowledge is contained in the *Vedas*, and their author, Vyāsadeva, accepts Kṛṣṇa as the Supreme Personality of Godhead, and Vyāsadeva's spiritual master, Nārada, also accepts Kṛṣṇa as such. Nārada's spiritual master, Brahmā, accepts Kṛṣṇa not only as the Supreme Person but the supreme controller as well—*īśvaraḥ paramaḥ kṛṣṇaḥ:* "The supreme controller is Kṛṣṇa."

There is no one in the creation who can claim that he is not controlled. Everyone, regardless of how important or powerful, has a controller over his head. Kṛṣṇa, however, has no controller; therefore He is God. He is the controller of everyone, but there is no one superior to Him, no one to control Him; nor is there anyone equal to Him, no one to share His platform of absolute control. This may sound very strange, for there are many so-called gods nowadays. Indeed, gods have become very cheap, being especially imported from India. People in other countries are fortunate that gods are not manufactured there, but in India gods are manufactured practically every day. We often hear that God is coming to Los Angeles or New York and that people are gathering to receive Him, etc. But Kṛṣṇa is not the type of God manufactured in a mystic factory. No. He was not *made* God, but He *is* God.

We should know then on the basis of authority that behind this gigantic material nature, the cosmic manifestation, there is God—Kṛṣṇa—and that He is accepted by all Vedic authorities. Acceptance of authority is not new for us; everyone accepts authority in some form or another. For education we go to a teacher or to a school or simply learn from our father and mother. They are all authorities, and our nature is to learn from them. In our childhood we asked, "Father, what is this?" and father would say, "This is a pen," "These are spectacles," or "This is a table." In this way from the very beginnings of life a child learns from his father and mother. He learns the names of things and the basic relations of one thing to another by questioning his parents. A good father and mother never cheat when their son inquires from them; they give exact and correct information. Similarly, if we get spiritual information from an authority and if the authority is not a cheater, then our knowledge is perfect. If we attempt to reach conclusions by dint of our own speculative powers, however, we are subject to fall into error. The process of induction, by which, reasoning from particular facts or individual cases, one can arrive at a general conclusion, is never a perfect process. Because we are limited and our experience is limited, it will always remain imperfect.

If we receive information from the perfect source, Kṛṣṇa, and if we repeat that information, then what we are speaking can also be accepted as perfect and authoritative. The process of *paramparā* or disciplic succession is this very process of hearing from Kṛṣṇa or from authorities who have accepted Kṛṣṇa and repeating exactly what they have said. In *Bhagavad-gītā* Kṛṣṇa recommends this process of knowledge:

evaṁ paramparā-prāptam
imaṁ rājarṣayo viduḥ

"This supreme science was thus received through the chain of disciplic succession, and the saintly kings understood it in that way." (Bg. 4.2)

Formerly knowledge was passed down by great saintly kings who were the authorities. In previous ages, however, these kings were *ṛṣis*—great learned scholars and devotees—and because they were not ordinary men the government which they headed worked very nicely. There are many instances in Vedic civilization of kings who attained perfection as devotees of God. For example, Dhruva Mahārāja went to the forest to search out God and by practice of severe penance and austerity found God within six months. Although he was only a five-year-old prince with a very delicate body, he was successful because he followed the directions of his spiritual master, Nārada. The first month Dhruva Mahārāja was in the forest, he simply ate some fruits and vegetables once every three days and drank a little water every six days. He finally restricted his inhalation of air and stood for six months on one leg only. After he executed these severe austerities for half a year, God became manifest before him, eye to eye. It is not necessary for us to practice such severe austerities, but simply by following in the footsteps of Vedic authorities we also can see God eye to eye. This vision of God is the perfection of life.

The Kṛṣṇa consciousness process is based on austerity, but it is not very difficult. There are restrictions governing eating and sex life (only *prasādam,* food first offered to Kṛṣṇa, is taken, and sex is restricted to married life), and there are other regulations which facilitate and foster spiritual realization.

It is not possible in these days to imitate Dhruva Mahārāja, but by following certain basic Vedic principles, we can make advancement in spiritual consciousness, Kṛṣṇa consciousness. As we advance, we become perfect in knowledge. What is the use in becoming a scientist or a philosopher if we cannot say what our next life will be? A realized student of Kṛṣṇa consciousness can very easily say what his next life is, what God is, what the living entity is and what his relationship with God is. His knowledge is perfect because it is coming from perfect books of knowledge such as *Bhagavad-gītā* and *Śrīmad-Bhāgavatam.*

This, then, is the process of Kṛṣṇa consciousness. It is very easy, and anyone can adopt it and make his life perfect. If someone says, "I'm not educated at all, and I cannot read books," he is still not disqualified. He can still perfect his life by simply chanting the *mahāmantra:* Hare Kṛṣṇa, Hare Kṛṣṇa, Kṛṣṇa Kṛṣṇa, Hare Hare/ Hare Rāma, Hare Rāma, Rāma Rāma, Hare Hare. Kṛṣṇa has given us a tongue and two ears, and we may be surprised to know that Kṛṣṇa is realized through the ears and tongue, not through the eyes. By hearing His message, we learn to control the tongue, and after the tongue is controlled, the other senses follow. Of all the senses, the tongue is the most voracious and difficult to control, but it can be controlled simply by chanting Hare Kṛṣṇa and tasting Kṛṣṇa *prasādam,* food offered to Kṛṣṇa.

We cannot understand Kṛṣṇa by sensual perception or by speculation. It is not possible, for Kṛṣṇa is so great that He is beyond our sensual range. But He can be understood by surrender. Kṛṣṇa therefore recommends this process:

sarva-dharmān parityajya
mām ekaṁ śaraṇaṁ vraja
ahaṁ tvāṁ sarva-pāpebhyo
mokṣayiṣyāmi mā śucaḥ

"Give up all varieties of religiousness, and just surrender unto Me; and in return I shall protect you from all sinful reactions. Therefore, you have nothing to fear." (Bg. 18.66)

Unfortunately, our disease is that we are rebellious–we automatically resist authority. Yet although we say that we don't want authority, nature is so strong that it forces authority upon us. We are forced to accept the authority of nature. What can be more pathetic than a man who claims to answer to no authority but who follows his senses blindly wherever they lead him? Our false claim to independence is simply foolishness. We are all under authority, yet we say that we don't want authority. This is called *māyā*, illusion. We do, however, have a certain independence–we can choose to be under the authority of our senses or the authority of Kṛṣṇa. The best and ultimate authority is Kṛṣṇa, for He is our eternal well-wisher, and He always speaks for our benefit. Since we have to accept some authority, why not accept His? Simply by hearing of His glories from *Bhagavad-gītā* and *Śrīmad-Bhāgavatam* and by chanting His names–Hare Kṛṣṇa–we can swiftly perfect our lives.

2/Getting Out the Material Mire

Our subject matter is most sublime: the glorification of the holy name of God. This subject was discussed by Mahārāja Parīkṣit and Śukadeva Gosvāmī, who noted that a *brāhmaṇa,* who was very fallen and addicted to all kinds of sinful activities, was saved simply by chanting the holy names of Kṛṣṇa. This is found in the Sixth Canto of *Śrīmad-Bhāgavatam,* an epic work by Vyāsadeva describing the pastimes of Lord Kṛṣṇa and elaborating on the philosophy of Kṛṣṇa consciousness.

In the Fifth Canto of *Śrīmad-Bhāgavatam,* the universal planetary systems are very fully explained. Within the universe there are lower, middle and higher planetary systems. Actually, not only the *Bhāgavatam* but all religious scriptures contain descriptions of hellish or lower planetary systems and heavenly or higher systems. *Śrīmad-Bhāgavatam* gives evidence of where these planets are and indicates how far they are from this planet, just as astronomers have calculated how far the moon and other heavenly bodies are from earth. Similarly, the *Bhāgavatam* contains descriptions of the various planets.

Even on this planet we experience different climatic conditions. In temperate countries such as the United States, the climate is different from that of a tropical country like India. Just as there are environmental differences on this planet, there are other planets which have far different atmospheres and environments. After hearing a description of such planets from Śukadeva Gosvāmī, Parīkṣit Mahārāja said:

adhuneha mahā-bhāga yathaiva narakān naraḥ
nānograyātanān neyāt tan me vyākhyātum arhasi

"Sir, I have heard from you about the hellish planets. Men who are very sinful are sent to those planets." (*Bhāg.* 6.1.6)

Parīkṣit Mahārāja was a Vaiṣṇava (devotee), and a Vaiṣṇava always feels compassion for others' distress. For instance, when Lord Jesus Christ appeared, he was greatly aggrieved by the miserable conditions of the people. Regardless of the country or sect to which they belong, all Vaiṣṇavas or devotees—any people who are God conscious or Kṛṣṇa conscious—are thus compassionate. Therefore to blaspheme a Vaiṣṇava, a preacher of God's glories, is a great offense.

Kṛṣṇa never tolerates offenses committed at the lotus feet of a pure Vaiṣṇava. A Vaiṣṇava, however, is always ready to forgive such offenses. *Kṛpāmbudhi:* A Vaiṣṇava is an ocean of mercy. *Vāñcā-kalpa-taru:* Everyone has desires, but a Vaiṣṇava can fulfill all desires. *Kalpa-taru* refers to a tree in the spiritual world which is called a wish-fulfilling tree. In this material world a particular type of fruit can only be gotten from a particular type of tree, but in

Kṛṣṇaloka, as well as in all the other planets in the spiritual sky, all the trees are spiritual and will yield whatever one desires. That is described in the *Brahma-saṁhitā (cintāmaṇi prakara-sadmasu kalpa-vṛkṣa).* A pure Vaiṣṇava is compared to such a wish-fulfilling tree, for he can bestow a matchless gift upon a sincere disciple—Kṛṣṇa consciousness.

A Vaiṣṇava is addressed as *mahā-bhāga,* which means "fortunate." One who becomes a Vaiṣṇava and is God conscious is understood to be greatly fortunate. Lord Caitanya Mahāprabhu, the chief exponent of Kṛṣṇa consciousness in this age, has explained that the living entities in various planetary systems all over the universe are rotating in different species of life. A living entity can go wherever he likes—to heaven or to hell—simply by preparing himself for either place. There are many heavenly planets, many hellish planets, and many species of life. *Padma Purāṇa* estimates the species of life to be 8,400,000, and the living entity is rotating or wandering through these species and creating bodies according to his mentality in his present life. "As you sow, so shall you reap," is the law that governs here. Caitanya Mahāprabhu says that out of these numberless living entities who are transmigrating in the material world, one may be fortunate enough to take to Kṛṣṇa consciousness. Kṛṣṇa consciousness is being distributed freely everywhere, yet not everyone takes to it, especially in this age of Kali. Because of this, *Śrīmad-Bhāgavatam* characterizes people in the age of Kali as unfortunate. Therefore Caitanya

Mahāprabhu says that only those who are fortunate take to this Kṛṣṇa consciousness and thus attain a pleasant and blissful life of knowledge.

It is the duty of a Vaiṣṇava to go from door to door to try to get unfortunate people to accept good fortune. A Vaiṣṇava thinks, "How can these people be delivered from their hellish life?" That was also Mahārāja Parīkṣit's inquiry. "Sir," he said, "you have described that because of one's sinful activities he is put into a hellish condition of life or in a hellish planetary system. Now, what are the methods by which such a person can be saved?" This is a very important question. When a Vaiṣṇava comes, when God Himself comes, or when God's sons or His very confidential devotees come, their only mission is to save sinful men who are suffering. They have knowledge of how to do this. When Prahlāda Mahārāja met Lord Nṛsiṁhadeva, he said:

naivodvije para duratyaya-vaitaraṇyās
tvadvīrya-gāyana-mahāmṛta-magna-cittaḥ
śoce tato vimukha-cetasa indriyārtha-
māyā-sukhāya bharam udvahato vimūḍhān
(*Bhāg.* 7.9.43)

"My dear Lord," Prahlāda began, "I am not very anxious for my own deliverance." At this point we may contrast this attitude with that of the Māyāvādī philosophers who are very careful that their personal salvation is never interrupted. They often think, "If I go to preach and associate with others, I may fall down, and my realization will be finished." Therefore they do not come forward to preach. Only the Vaiṣṇavas come, even at the risk of falldown—but they do not fall down. A Vaiṣṇava is even willing to go to hell to deliver conditioned souls. This is also Prahlāda Mahārāja's mission. He went on to say: "I am not very anxious about living in this material world. I have no anxiety for myself because somehow or other I have been trained to be Kṛṣṇa conscious always." Because Prahlāda was Kṛṣṇa conscious, he was confident that in his next life he was going to Kṛṣṇa. It is stated in *Bhagavad-gītā* that if one executes the regulated principles of Kṛṣṇa consciousness carefully, it is certain that he will reach the supreme destination in his next life. Prahlāda Mahārāja continues: "There is only one source of anxiety for me. I am anxious for those who are not Kṛṣṇa conscious. For myself I have no anxiety, but I am thinking of them." And why aren't people Kṛṣṇa conscious? *Māyā-sukhāya bharam udvahato vimūḍhān.* The rascals have created a humbug civilization for temporary happiness.

Māyā-sukhāya. Actually this is a fact. We have succeeded in creating a humbug civilization. Every year so many cars are being manufactured, and for that purpose so many roads have to be excavated, prepared and repaired. This creates problems after problems, and therefore it is *māyā-sukhāya,* illusory happiness. We are trying to manufacture some way to be happy, but we only succeed in creating other problems. The United States has the world's largest number of cars, but that does not solve any problems. We have manufactured cars to help solve the problems of life, but we often experience that this also creates other problems. Once we create cars, we must travel thirty or forty miles just to meet our friends or go to a doctor. We can even go from New York to Boston in less than an hour by plane, but it takes even longer than that just to get to the airport. This situation is called *māyā-sukhāya. Māyā* means false, illusory. We try to create a very comfortable situation, but we only succeed in creating another uncomfortable situation. This is the way of the material world; if we are not satisfied by the natural comforts offered by God and nature, and we want to create artificial comforts, then we have to create discomfort also. Most people, ignorant of this fact, think that they are creating a very comfortable situation, but in actuality they end up traveling fifty miles to go to the office to earn a livelihood and fifty miles to come back.

Due to such conditions, Prahlāda Mahārāja says that these *vimūḍhas,* materialistic persons, have unnecessarily burdened themselves simply for temporary happiness. *Vimūḍhān, māyā-sukhāya bharam udvahato.* Therefore in Vedic civilization it is recommended that one free himself from material life, take *sannyāsa,* the renounced order, and execute devotional service with no anxiety.

The taking of the renounced order, however, is not always necessary. If one can execute Kṛṣṇa consciousness in family life, that is also recommended. Although Bhaktivinoda Ṭhākura was a family man and magistrate, he still executed devotional service most excellently. Dhruva Mahārāja and

Prahlāda Mahārāja were also *gṛhasthas,* householders, but they trained themselves in such a way that even as householders they were not faced with interruptions in their service. Therefore Prahlāda Mahārāja said, "I have learned the art of always remaining in Kṛṣṇa consciousness." What is that art? *Tvad-vīrya-gāyana-mahāmṛta-magna-cittaḥ:* simply glorifying the victorious activities and pastimes of the Lord. The word *vīrya* means "very heroic." By reading *Śrīmad-Bhāgavatam,* we can come to understand that Kṛṣṇa's activities, His fame, His associates and everything else about Him are all heroic. In this connection, Prahlāda Mahārāja said: "I am certain that wherever I go, I can glorify Your heroic activities and be saved. There is no question of my falling down, but I am simply anxious for those who have created a type of civilization in which they are always busy working hard. I am thinking of them." Prahlāda further says:

prāyeṇa deva munayaḥ sva-vimukti-kāmā
maunaṁ caranti vijane na parārtha-niṣṭhāḥ
naitān vihāya kṛpaṇān vimumukṣa eko
nānyaṁ tvadasya śaraṇaṁ bhramato 'nupaśye

"My dear Lord, there are many saintly persons and sages who are very interested in their own liberation. They live in solitary places like the Himalayan mountains, they do not talk to anyone, and they are always afraid of mixing with ordinary people in the cities and becoming disturbed or maybe even falling down. They think, 'Better let me save myself.' I regret that these great saintly persons do not come to the cities where people have manufactured a civilization based on constant hard work. Such saints are not very compassionate, but I am anxious for these fallen people who are unnecessarily working so hard simply for the gratification of the senses." (*Bhāg.* 7.9.44)

Even if there were some point in working that hard, such people do not know what it is. All they know is the sex urge and the brothels that gratify this urge. However, Prahlāda Mahārāja has compassion for such people: *naitān vihāya kṛpaṇān vimumukṣa eko.* "My Lord, I do not need salvation alone. Unless I take all these fools with me, I shall not go." Thus he refused to go into the kingdom of God without taking all the fallen souls with him. This is a Vaiṣṇava. *Nānyaṁ tvadasya śaraṇaṁ bhramato 'nupaśye:* "I simply want to teach them how to surrender unto You. That's all. That is my goal."

Surrender is thus emphasized because a Vaiṣṇava knows that as soon as he surrenders, the path is clear.

naivodvije para duratyaya-vaitaraṇyās
tvad-vīrya-gāyana-mahāmṛta-magna-cittaḥ

"Somehow or other, let them all bow down before Kṛṣṇa." This is a very simple method. All one has to do is bow down before Kṛṣṇa with faith and say, "My Lord Kṛṣṇa, I was forgetful of You for so long, for so many lives. Now I have come to consciousness of You. Please accept me." That is all. If one simply learns this technique and sincerely surrenders himself to the Lord, his path is immediately opened. This is the aim of a real Vaiṣṇava.

A Vaiṣṇava is always thinking about how the fallen conditioned souls can be delivered and is always involved in making plans to do so. The Gosvāmīs, the chief disciples of Lord Caitanya Mahāprabhu, were such Vaiṣṇavas, and were thus described by Śrīnivāsa Ācārya:

nānā-śāstra-vicāraṇaika-nipuṇau sad-dharma-
saṁsthāpakau
lokānāṁ hitakāriṇau tribhuvane mānyau
śaraṇyākarau
rādhā-kṛṣṇa-padāravinda-bhajanānandena
mattālikau
vande rūpa-sanātanau raghuyugau śrī-jīva-
gopālakau

"The six Gosvāmīs—Śrī Sanātana Gosvāmī, Śrī Rūpa Gosvāmī, Śrī Raghunātha Bhaṭṭa Gosvāmī, Śrī Raghunātha Dāsa Gosvāmī, Śrī Jīva Gosvāmī and Śrī Gopāla Bhaṭṭa Gosvāmī—are very expert in scrutinizingly studying all the revealed scriptures with the purpose of establishing eternal religious principles for the benefit of all human beings. They are always absorbed in the mood of the *gopīs* and are engaged in the transcendental loving service of Rādhā and Kṛṣṇa."

With similar Vaiṣṇava compassion, Parīkṣit Mahārāja told Śukadeva Gosvāmī: "You have just described the different types of hellish life. Now, tell me how those who are suffering can be delivered. Kindly explain this to me." *Adhuneha mahā-bhāga yathaiva narakān naraḥ nānograyātanān neyāt tan me.* The word *naraḥ* refers to human beings, or those who are fallen. *Narakān naraḥ nānograyātanān neyāt tan me:* "How can they be delivered from their fierce miseries and horrible pains?" That is typical of a Vaiṣṇava heart. Mahārāja Parīkṣit also said, "Somehow or other they have fallen down to a hellish life, but that does not mean that they should remain in that condition. There must be some means by which they can be delivered, so kindly explain those means."

Śukadeva Gosvāmī replied:

na ced ihaivāpacitiṁ yathāṁhasaḥ
kṛtasya kuryān mana-ukti-pāṇibhiḥ
dhruvaṁ sa vai pretya narakān upaiti
ye kīrtitā me bhavatas tigma-yātanāḥ

"Yes, I have already described various hellish conditions typical of a severe and painful life. The point is that one has to counteract such a life." (*Bhāg.* 6.1.7)

How can this be done? There are various ways in which sinful activities can be committed. One is by the mind. If a person thinks of committing some sinful activity and thus makes a plan—"I shall kill that man"—that is also considered to be sinful. When the mind is thinking, feeling and willing, then there is action. In certain areas of the United States, a dog owner is responsible according to law if his dog barks at someone passing on the road. Although the dog simply barks, the owner is held responsible. The dog is not responsible because it is an animal, but because the owner of the animal has made the dog his best friend, he is responsible by law. Similarly, just as the barking of a dog may be considered unlawful, offensive speech may also be considered sinful, for it is just like barking. The point is that sinful activities can be committed in so many ways—one may think of them, or one may speak sinfully, or one may actually commit a sin. In any case, they are all considered sinful activities. *Dhruvaṁ sa vai pretya narakān upaiti:* One has to suffer punishment for such activities.

People do not believe in a next life because they want to avoid botheration and punishment, but the next life cannot be avoided. It is a well known fact that we must act according to law, or we will be punished. If one commits criminal activities, the state will punish him. Sometimes, however, a criminal may escape punishment by the state, but this is not the case with God's law. One can cheat others, commit theft and hide, thereby saving himself from the punishment of the state, but one cannot save himself from the superior law, the law of nature. It is very difficult because there are many witnesses: the daylight is witness, the moonlight is witness, and Kṛṣṇa is the supreme witness. Thus one cannot say, "I am committing this sin, but no one can see me." Kṛṣṇa is the supreme witness sitting within the heart, and He not only notes what one is thinking and doing, but He also gives the living entity facility. If one wants to do something in order to satisfy his senses, Kṛṣṇa gives all facility. This is stated in *Bhagavad-gītā. Sarvasya cāhaṁ hṛdi sanniviṣṭaḥ:* "I am sitting in everyone's heart." *Mattaḥ smṛtir jñānam apohanaṁ ca:* "From Me come remembrance, knowledge and forgetfulness."

In this way Kṛṣṇa gives us a chance. If we want Kṛṣṇa, He will give us a chance to have Him, and if we don't want Kṛṣṇa, He will give us a chance to forget Him. If we want to enjoy life forgetting Kṛṣṇa, forgetting God, Kṛṣṇa will give us all facility so that we can forget, but if we want to enjoy life in Kṛṣṇa consciousness, Kṛṣṇa will give us the chance to make progress. That is up to us. If we think that we can be happy without Kṛṣṇa consciousness, Kṛṣṇa does not object to that. *Yathecchasi tathā kuru.* After advising Arjuna, He simply said, "Now I have explained everything to you. Whatever you desire, you can do." Arjuna replied immediately, *kariṣye vacanaṁ tava:* "Now I shall execute Your order." That is Kṛṣṇa consciousness.

God does not interfere with our tiny independence. If we want to act according to the order of God, then He will help us. Even if one falls down sometimes, if one becomes sincere, thinking, "From this time I shall remain Kṛṣṇa conscious and execute His orders," then Kṛṣṇa will help him. In all respects, even if one falls down, he will be excused and given more intelligence. This intelligence will say, "Don't do this. Now go on with your duty." But if one wants to forget Kṛṣṇa, if he wants to become happy without Kṛṣṇa, the Lord will give so many chances to enable him to forget Him life after life.

Parīkṣit Mahārāja said: "It is not that if I say there is no God that there will be no God or that I will not be responsible for what I do." The atheists deny God due to their sinful activities. If they thought that there were a God, they would shudder at the thought of punishment; therefore they deny His existence. When rabbits are attacked by larger animals, they close their eyes and think, "I am not going to be killed," but they are killed anyway. Similarly, we may deny the existence of God and His laws, but still God and His laws are there. In the high court, one may say, "I don't care for the law of the government," but he will be forced to accept the government law. If one denies the state law, he will be put into prison and duly punished. Similarly, one may foolishly decry the existence of God by various means ("There is no God," or "I am God"), but ultimately one is responsible for all his actions, both good and bad.

According to the law of *karma,* or the law governing activities, if we act properly and perform pious activities, we are awarded by good fortune, and if we act sinfully we have to suffer. Therefore Śukadeva Gosvāmī says:

tasmāt puraivāśv iha pāpa-niṣkṛtau
yateta mṛtyor avipadyatātmanā
doṣasya dṛṣṭvā guru-lāghavaṁ yathā
bhiṣak cikitseta rujāṁ nidāna-vit

"You should know that you are responsible, and, according to the gravity of your sins, you should accept some type of atonement as described in the *śāstras* or scriptures."(*Bhāg.* 6.1.8)

Just as doctors are sought when one is diseased, according to the Vedic way of life there is a class of *brāhmaṇas* to whom one should go for prescribed atonement for sinful activities. There are different types of atonement. If a person commits a sin and counteracts it by penance, that is atonement. There are examples of this in the Christian Bible. Śukadeva says that one has to execute the prescribed atonement according to the gravity of his sinful activities. A physician may prescribe an expensive medicine or a cheap medicine according to the gravity of the disease. For a headache, he may simply prescribe an aspirin, but if there is some severe illness he may prescribe a surgical operation which will cost thousands of dollars. Similarly, sinful activities are diseases, so one should follow the prescribed cures to become healthy.

By accepting the chain of birth and death, the soul accepts a diseased condition. The soul is not subject to birth, death or disease because it is pure spirit. In *Bhagavad-gītā* Kṛṣṇa says that a soul has no birth (*na jāyate*) and that it has no death (*mriyate*).

na jāyate mriyate vā kadācin
nāyaṁ bhūtvā bhavitā vā na bhūyaḥ
ajo nityaḥ śāśvato 'yaṁ purāṇo
na hanyate hanyamāne śarīre

"For the soul there is never birth or death. Nor, having once been, does he ever cease to be. He is unborn, eternal, ever-existing, undying and primeval. He is not slain when the body is slain." (Bg. 2.20)

Modern civilization is in dire need of an educational system to give people instructions on what happens after death. In actuality the present educational system is most defective because unless one knows what happens after death, one dies like an animal. An animal does not know that he is subject to death or that he is going to have to take another body. Human life, however, should be more elevated. One should not simply be interested in the animalistic functions of eating, sleeping, defending and mating. A living entity may have an abundant supply of food for eating, or many nice buildings for sleeping, or good arrangements for sex life, or a good defense to protect him, but this does not mean that he is a human being. A civilization which is based on these activities should be known to be animalistic. Since animals are also interested in these functions, what is the difference between human life and animal life if a human being does not go beyond them?

The distinction can be made when a human being becomes inquisitive and asks, "Why have I been put into this miserable condition? Is there any remedy for it? Is there perpetual eternal life? I do not want to die, nor do I want to suffer. I want to live very happily and peacefully. Is there a chance for this? What is the method or science by which this can be achieved?" When these questions are asked, and steps are taken to answer them, our human civilization is the result. If the questions never arise, then that civilization should be known as animalistic.

Animals and animalistic human beings are simply interested in continuing the process of eating, sleeping, mating and defending, but in actuality this process is forced to break down. The fact is that there is no real defense because no one can protect himself from the hands of cruel death. For instance, Hiraṇyakaśipu, who wanted to live forever, underwent severe austerities, but he was foiled in the end by the Lord Himself in the form of a lion-man, Nṛsiṁhadeva, who killed Hiraṇyakaśipu with His claws. So-called scientists are now claiming that some time in the future we shall stop death by scientific methods, but this is simply another crazy utterance. Stopping death is not at all possible. We may make great advancements in scientific knowledge, but there is no scientific solution to the fourfold miseries of birth, death, old age and disease.

One who is intelligent should be eager to solve these four principal problems—birth, death, old age and disease. No one wants to die, but there is no remedy. Everyone has to die. Everyone is very anxious to stop the skyrocketing increase of population by employing contraceptive methods, but still birth is going on. There is no stoppage of death, and there is no stoppage of birth. Nor can diseases be stopped, nor can old age, despite all of the latest inventions in medicine.

One might think that he has solved all the problems of his life, but where is the solution to these four problems of birth, death, old age and disease? That solution is Kṛṣṇa consciousness. Every one of us is giving up his body at every moment, and the last phase of giving up this body is called death. But Kṛṣṇa also says:

janma karma ca me divyam
evaṁ yo vetti tattvataḥ
tyaktvā dehaṁ punar janma
naiti mām eti so 'rjuna

"One who knows the transcendental nature of My appearance and activities does not, upon leaving the body, take his birth again in this material world, but attains My eternal abode, O Arjuna." (Bg. 4.9)

What happens to such a person? *Mām eti*–He returns to Kṛṣṇa. If we are to go to Kṛṣṇa, we must prepare a spiritual body. That preparation is the process of Kṛṣṇa consciousness. If one keeps himself in Kṛṣṇa consciousness, he gradually prepares his next body, a spiritual body, which will carry him immediately to Kṛṣṇaloka, Kṛṣṇa's abode, and he will become happy living there perpetually and blissfully.

3/ Learning to Love

Contamination from sinful activity requires proportionate atonement. That is the prescription of the scriptures. Śukadeva Gosvāmī says that if one accepts atonement before death, in his next life he will not fall down. If he does not atone, he will carry with him the resultant reactions of his sinful activities and will have to suffer. According to law, if a man kills someone he must himself be killed. The idea of a life for a life is not a very new concept but can be found in the *Manu-saṁhitā,* the Vedic lawbook for mankind, where it is stated that when a king hangs the murderer, the murderer is actually benefited, for if he is not killed, he will carry the reaction for his murder and will have to suffer in so many ways.

The laws of nature are very subtle and are very diligently administered, although people do not know it. In the *Manu-saṁhitā* the concept of a life for a life is sanctioned, and it is actually observed throughout the world. Similarly, there are other laws which state that one cannot even kill an ant without being responsible. Since we cannot create, we have no right to kill any living entity, and therefore man-made laws that distinguish between killing a man and killing an animal are imperfect. Although there are imperfections in man-made laws, there cannot be defects in the laws of God. According to the laws of God, killing an animal is as punishable as killing a man. Those who draw distinctions between the two are concocting their own laws. Even in the Ten Commandments it is prescribed, "Thou shall not kill." This is a perfect law, but by discriminating and speculating men distort it. "I shall not kill man, but I shall kill animals." In this way people cheat themselves and inflict suffering on themselves and others. In any case, however, God's laws will not excuse such behavior.

Everyone is God's creature, although in different bodies or dresses. God is considered the one supreme father. A father may have many children, and some may be intelligent and others not very intelligent, but if an intelligent son tells his father, "My brother is not very intelligent; let me kill him," will the father agree? Simply because one son is not very intelligent and the other desires to kill him to avoid the burden, the father will never agree. Similarly, if God is the supreme father, why should He sanction the killing of animals who are also His sons? In *Bhagavad-gītā* God declares to Arjuna that all 8,400,000 species of living entities are His sons. "And I am their seed-giving father," the Lord says. Just as in ordinary material procreation the father gives the seed and the mother develops the body by supplying the necessary blood to the embryo, similarly, the living entities, parts and parcels of the supreme father, are impregnated by the Lord in material nature.

The dimension of the spirit soul is very minute and is given in the scriptures as *keśāgra*—one ten thousandth the portion of the tip of a hair. We can hardly imagine a very small point divided into thousands of parts. In other words, it is so minute that it cannot be perceived even by the most powerful microscope. Thus the dimension of the spiritual spark is so minute that it is invisible to mundane vision. All of this information is given in the scriptures, but because we do not have the proper vision, we cannot see. Although our material eyes cannot perceive the dimension of the soul, the soul is nonetheless within the body, and as soon as it departs, it takes another body according to its work.

One should always consider that behind all these activities is superior superintendence. The living entity works in the material world just as the office worker works at his job, and a service record is kept of his performance. The living entity does not know what the opinion of his superior is, but his service record is kept in the office nonetheless, and according to his activities he is awarded promotion or increment of pay, or sometimes he may be demoted or even fired. Similarly, for all our activities there are witnesses; therefore it is said in the scriptures that the living entities are under superior supervision and that they are rewarded and punished according to their work. Now we have human bodies, but in the next life we may not have them; we may have something else, better or lower. The type of body is decided by the living entity's superiors. Generally the living entity does not know the science of how the spirit soul transmigrates from one body to another.

The spirit soul transmigrates even in the duration of one life as the body changes. When the body is first manifest in the womb of the mother, it is very small, just like a pea, and it gradually develops nine holes—two eyes, two ears, two nostrils, one mouth, one genital, and one rectum. In this way the body develops, and as long as it needs to develop within the mother's womb, it remains there. When it is sufficiently developed to go outside, it comes out and grows. Growth entails changing of the body. This change cannot be understood because it is imperceivable to the living entity. In childhood we had small bodies which now no longer exist; therefore it can be said that we have changed our bodies. Similarly, because of the nature of material things, we have to change this body when it ceases to work. Every material thing deteriorates, and like a broken machine or an old piece of cloth the body becomes useless after a certain length of time.

Although this process of growth is always taking place, the educational system in modern universities, though considered advanced, unfortunately does not deal with this. Actually there is no education without spiritual knowledge. One can learn to earn bread, eat, sleep and mate without a formal education. Animals are not educated—they are not technicians, and they have no university degrees—but they are also eating, sleeping, mating and defending. If the educational system simply teaches these processes, it does not deserve the name of education. Real education enables us to understand what we are. As long as man does not develop his consciousness by understanding the truth of the self, all of his actions will be performed in the mode of ignorance. A human life is meant for victory over the laws of material nature. Actually, we are all trying to attain that victory in order to counteract the onslaught of material nature. The ultimate victory is to conquer birth, death, disease and old age, but we have neglected this important point.

If the educational system dealt with the proper utilization of what God is supplying, it would improve. All the fruits and grains we eat are given by God, who supplies food to all living entities. In *Śrīmad-Bhāgavatam* it is stated, *jīvo jīvasya jīvanam:* "One living entity is food for another." (*Bhāg.* 1.13.47) Animals without hands are food for animals with hands, such as ourselves. Animals with no legs are food for animals with four legs. Grass is a living entity, but it has no legs with which to move, and thus it is eaten by cows and other animals. Such non-moving entities are food for moving animals, and in this way the world is in a constant struggle between exploiters and exploited. The weaker is exploited by the stronger; this is nature's law. Traditionally, Vaiṣṇavas, or devotees of Kṛṣṇa, do not eat meat. This is not just for the sake of vegetarianism, but for the furtherance of God consciousness. In order to become God conscious, one must follow some rules and regulations. Of course one has to eat, but the proposal is that one should eat remnants of foodstuffs that are offered to Kṛṣṇa. This is also the philosophy of *Bhagavad-gītā*, wherein Kṛṣṇa says:

patraṁ puṣpaṁ phalaṁ toyaṁ
yo me bhaktyā prayacchati
tad ahaṁ bhakty-upahṛtam
aśnāmi prayatātmanaḥ

"If one offers Me with love and devotion a leaf, a flower, fruit or water, I will accept it." (Bg. 9.26)

It is not that Kṛṣṇa is hungry and is begging food from us. The purpose of this offering is to create a loving transaction. Kṛṣṇa wants this transaction: "You love Me, and I'll love you." As God, Kṛṣṇa's energy creates and sustains everything, so why should He beg a leaf, a fruit and a little water from us? He will be very pleased, however, if we offer Him a piece of fruit, a leaf and water with love, saying, "Kṛṣṇa, I am so poor that I cannot secure anything. I have secured this fruit and a leaf. Kindly accept them." Such an offering would make Kṛṣṇa very glad. If He eats what we offer, our life will be successful, for we will actually make friends with Kṛṣṇa. Fruit, flowers and water can be secured practically in any part of the world by any man, poor or rich, and can be offered. We should remember then that it is not vegetarianism which is important, nor is it that God is in need of anything. The important point is that we simply have to try to learn how to love Kṛṣṇa.

Love begins with this give and take. We give something to our lover, he gives something to us, and in this way love develops. When we create any loving transaction with any boy or girl, man or woman, we give and take. Thus Kṛṣṇa is teaching us how to give and take. Kṛṣṇa is begging us: "Try to love Me. Learn how to love Me. Offer something to Me."

"Sir," we may say, "I have nothing to give You."

"Oh, you cannot collect a piece of fruit, a flower, a leaf or a little water?"

"Oh yes, why not? Anyone can collect this."

This, then, is the method of Krsna consciousness which allows one to make friends with Kṛṣṇa. We can enter into any number of relationships with Kṛṣṇa. We can become a direct servant of Kṛṣṇa, or in the highest stages we can become Kṛṣṇa's father, mother or lover. Kṛṣṇa is prepared to establish a loving relationship with all living entities. In actuality this relationship is already there because He is the supreme father and we are His parts and parcels. Because the son is part of the body of the father, the relationship between them cannot be broken; it may be forgotten for some time, but as soon as one recognizes his father or son, immediately affection develops. Similarly, we are eternally related to Kṛṣṇa, but at the present moment this relationship is simply forgotten or suppressed. Consequently,we think that we have no relationship with Kṛṣṇa, but this is not a fact. Because we are integral with Him, because we are part and parcel of Him, our relationship with Him is eternal. That relationship simply has to be revived, and that revival is this process of Kṛṣṇa consciousness.

At present we are under the sway of a different consciousness. One person is thinking that he is Indian, another is thinking that he is American, and someone else is thinking, "I am this," or "I am that." In this way we create so many artificial identities, but our actual identity should be, "I am Kṛṣṇa's." When we think in this way, we are thinking in Kṛṣṇa consciousness. Only in this way can universal love among all living entities be established. Kṛṣṇa is related to everyone as eternal father, and consequently when we establish a Kṛṣṇa conscious relationship, we become related to everyone. When one marries, he automatically establishes a relationship with the spouse's family. Similarly, if we reestablish our original relationship with Kṛṣṇa, we will establish our true relationship with everyone else. That is the ground for real universal love. Universal love is artificial and cannot endure unless we establish our relationship with the center. One is American if he is born in America, and thus other Americans become members of his family, but if he is born elsewhere, he has no relationship with Americans. On the mundane platform all relationships are relative. Our relationship with Kṛṣṇa, however, is eternal and not subject to time and circumstance. When we reestablish our relationship with Kṛṣṇa, the questions of universal brotherhood, justice, peace and prosperity will be answered. There is no possibility of realizing these higher ideals without Kṛṣṇa. If the central point is missing, how can there be brotherhood and peace?

In *Bhagavad-gītā* the peace formula is clearly given. We have to understand that Kṛṣṇa is the only enjoyer. The consciousness of this is developed in a Kṛṣṇa conscious temple where the central point of all activities is Kṛṣṇa. All cooking is carried on for Kṛṣṇa, not for one's own purposes. Ultimately we shall eat the *prasādam* (offered food), but when we cook we should think that we are cooking for Kṛṣṇa and not for ourselves. When the members of a temple go into the streets, they do not do so for their own sake but to distribute Kṛṣṇa conscious literatures in order to make people aware of Kṛṣṇa's presence. All monies acquired are spent for Kṛṣṇa, in spreading His message in so many ways. Such a style of life, in which everything is done for Kṛṣṇa, promotes the development of Kṛṣṇa consciousness within the living entity. Our activities may remain the same; we simply have to understand that we are acting for Kṛṣṇa and not for our personal satisfaction. In this way we can come to our original consciousness and be happy. Unless one is established in his original consciousness, which is Kṛṣṇa consciousness, he is certain to be crazy to some degree. Everyone who is not Kṛṣṇa conscious is to be considered crazy because he exists on a platform which is temporary and transient. Since we as living entities are eternal, temporary activities are not our concern. Our engagements should be eternal because we are eternal, and that eternal engagement is the rendering of service to Kṛṣṇa in love.

Kṛṣṇa is the supreme eternal, and we are subordinate eternals. Kṛṣṇa is the supreme living entity, and we are subordinate living entities. The finger is part and parcel of the total body, and its eternal function is to serve the body. Indeed, that is the very purpose for the finger, and if it cannot serve the whole body, it is diseased or useless. Similarly, as part and parcel we have to serve Kṛṣṇa and be subordinate to Him because as the supreme father He supplies all our necessities. Such a life of subordination to Kṛṣṇa is a normal life and is a life of actual liberation. Those who try to deny Kṛṣṇa and live outside of any relationship to Him are actually leading a sinful life.

Śukadeva Gosvāmī and Mahārāja Parīkṣit discussed this subject, and Parīkṣit Mahārāja was anxious to know how the conditioned souls could be saved from their hellish lives. It is the natural desire of a Vaiṣṇava to save suffering humanity. Generally others do not care whether people suffer or not, but a Vaiṣṇava, a devotee of the Lord, is always thinking of how to alleviate the fallen condition of the people. Christians believe that through His crucifixion Lord Jesus Christ assimilated all the sinful activities of the world's people. A devotee of the Lord is always thinking of how to assimilate the sufferings of others. A similar devotee was Vāsudeva Datta, who was Lord Caitanya's associate. He told the Lord: "Now that You have come, kindly deliver all people on this earth and take them to Vaikuṇṭha, the spiritual world. And if You think that they are so sinful that they cannot be delivered, please transfer all their sins unto me. I shall suffer for them." This is a Vaiṣṇava's mercy. However, it is not that Jesus Christ or Vāsudeva Datta should make a contract for our sins and that we should go on committing them, for this is a most heinous proposal. A Vaiṣṇava or devotee may suffer for all humanity, but the human race or a particular devotee's disciples should not take advantage of this facility and continue to commit sins. One should, rather, realize that since Lord Jesus Christ or Vāsudeva Datta suffered for him, he should stop committing sins.

Factually everyone is responsible for his own sinful activities. Therefore Śukadeva Gosvāmī recommends, *tasmāt puraivāśv iha pāpa-niṣkṛtau:* In order to free oneself from all the reactions of sinful activities, as long as one is embodied, he should atone. *Yateta mṛtyor avipadyatātmanā doṣasya dṛṣṭvā guru-lāghavaṁ yathā bhiṣak cikitseta rujāṁ nidāna-vit.* According to one's sinful activities, he should accept a program of atonement. As mentioned before, there are different atonements for different sinful activities. In any case, before death one should perform atonement so that he does not carry sinful activities into his next life and have to suffer then. If some atonement for our sinful activities is not performed, nature will not excuse us. We will have to suffer the effects of our sins in the next life. Such bondage to one's material activities is called *karma-bandhanaḥ.*

yajñārthāt karmaṇo 'nyatra
loko 'yaṁ karma-bandhanaḥ
tad-arthaṁ karma kaunteya
mukta-saṅgaḥ samācara

"Work done as a sacrifice for Viṣṇu has to be performed, otherwise work binds one to this material world. Therefore, O son of Kuntī, perform your prescribed duties for His satisfaction, and in that way you will always remain unattached and free from bondage." (Bg. 3.9)

One may kill an animal to enjoy eating it, but he will be bound by such an action. Thus in one's next life he will become a cow or a goat, and the cow or goat will become a man and eat him. This is the Vedic statement, and as with all Vedic statements, one may believe it or not. Unfortunately, at present people are educated in such a way that they do not believe in the next life. Indeed, it seems that the more "educated" one becomes, the less he believes in God, in God's law, in the next life and in sinful and pious activities. Thus modern education is simply preparing men to become animals. If there is no education to teach a human being what he is and whether or not he is this body, he remains no better than an ass. An ass also thinks, "I am this body," as do other animals. Thus if a man thinks in the same way, how is he different from any other animal? *Śrīmad-Bhāgavatam* states:

yasyātma-buddhiḥ kuṇape tridhātuke
sva-dhīḥ kalatrādiṣu bhauma ijyadhīḥ
yat tīrtha-buddhiḥ salile na karhicij
janeṣv abhijñeṣu sa eva gokharaḥ

"For one who accepts the body–which is made of three elements–as his self, who has an affinity for intimate bodily relationships with his wife and children, who considers his land worshipable and who accepts the waters of holy places of pilgrimage but does not take advantage of the knowledge of the saintly persons there, is to be considered to be in illusion and no better than an ass or a cow." (*Bhāg.* 10.84.13) According to *Āyur Veda,* the material body is composed of three elements, *kapha-pitta-vātaiḥ*–mucus, bile and air. Within the body there is complex machinery which transforms food into liquid. There are so many complicated bodily processes going on, but what do we know of them? We say, "This is my body," but what do we know about this body? Some people even claim, "I am God," but they do not even know what is going on within their own bodies.

The body is a bag of stool, urine, blood and bones. If one believes that intelligence comes out of stool, urine, blood and bones, he is a fool. Can we create intelligence by mixing stool, urine, bones and blood? Nonetheless people still think, "I am this body." Therefore the scriptures say that whoever accepts this body as the self and accepts the bodily relations of wife, children and family as his own, is illusioned. The word *kalatra* means wife, and *ādi* means beginning. Because a man feels alone, he accepts a wife, and immediately there are children and then grandchildren. In this way there is expansion. *Strī* means "that which expands," so *kalatrādiṣu* means "expansions of the self," beginning from the wife. The word *bhauma* refers to the land of one's birth, which the ignorant consider worshipable *(ijyadhīḥ)*. People are willing to give up their lives for the land where they were born, but they do not know that land, body, wife, children, country and society really have nothing to do with them. We are spirit soul *(ahaṁ brahmāsmi)*. This is realization of knowledge, and when we come to this point of knowledge, we become happy.

brahma-bhūtaḥ prasannātmā
na śocati na kāṅkṣati
samaḥ sarveṣu bhūteṣu
mad-bhaktiṁ labhate parām

"He who is transcendentally situated at once realizes the Supreme Brahman. He never laments nor desires anything. He is equally disposed to all the living entities, and in that state he achieves pure devotional service unto Me." (Bg. 18.54) One immediately becomes jolly *(prasannātmā)* when he comes to understand "I am spirit soul. I am Brahman. I am not this matter." The sign of this joy is that one no longer feels hankering and lamentation. Within this world everyone is subject to lamentation for that which is lost and hankering for that which must be gained, but real gain is to understand oneself and to know one's own identity.

As long as we maintain the bodily conception of life, we have to abide by the laws of material nature as well as the laws of the state and all other laws. Thus this body is called conditional, because it is subject to different conditions. There are varieties of conditions, and regardless of the condition to which we are subjected, we are responsible. If we do not atone for sinful activities committed while in this body, we will have to suffer in the next body because we will get another body according to *karma (yaṁ yaṁ vāpi smaran bhāvaṁ tyajaty ante kalevaram).* That is nature's law. Śukadeva Gosvāmī therefore recommends that one undergo atonement according to the gravity of his sinful activities. One must follow the methods of atonement prescribed in the *śāstras,* otherwise there is no rescue.

Parīkṣit Mahārāja, who was very intelligent, said, "By atonement one can become free from sinful activity, but suppose a man has committed murder and then is killed—the sinful reaction of his murder is thus neutralized, but it is not guaranteed that in his next life he'll not kill another man." Thus Parīkṣit Mahārāja noted that after atoning, people commit the same sins again. If a man is diseased, the physician may give him medicine and cure him, but it does not guarantee that he will not be attacked again by the same disease. Venereal diseases are often contacted again and again, despite cures, and a thief may steal again and again, despite being repeatedly being thrown into jail. Why is this? Therefore Parīkṣit Mahārāja noted that although atonement may be good for counteracting sinful activities already committed, it does not prevent those sins from being committed again. Everyone can see that a man who commits murder is punished, but seeing this is not enough to deter one from killing. In every scripture and in every lawbook man is warned not to kill, yet no one is concerned with these laws. What is the remedy for this? *Dṛṣṭa-śrutābhyāṁ yat pāpaṁ.* By practical experience and by hearing from authorities, everyone knows what sinful activity is, and no one can say, "I do not know what sin is." What is the value of atonement if one commits the same sin again and again after atoning? *Kvacin nivartate 'bhadrāt kvacic carati tat punaḥ prāyaścittam ato 'pārthaṁ manye kuñjara-śaucavat* (*Bhāg.* 6.1.9). When one is being punished, he thinks, "What a mistake I have made! I shall not commit this sin anymore." But as soon as he is out of danger, he again commits the same sin.

Habit is second nature; it is very difficult to break. *Śvā yadi kriyate rājā/ tat kiṁ nāśnāty upānaham (Hitopadeśa):* One may seat a dog on a royal throne, but as soon as he sees a shoe, he will immediately jump down and run after it simply because he is a dog. The canine qualities are there, and they cannot be changed simply by putting the dog on a throne. Similarly, we have acquired material qualities by associating with the three modes of material nature—*sattva guṇa, rajo guṇa* and *tamo guṇa*—and our habits are formed by association with these three qualities, which are the qualities of goodness, passion and ignorance. If, however, we disassociate ourselves from the three modes of material nature, our real spiritual nature is invoked. That is the process of Kṛṣṇa consciousness. If one is Kṛṣṇa conscious, there is no chance of his associating with the three modes of material nature, and when one is conscious of Kṛṣṇa, one's spiritual nature is automatically invoked. That is the secret. Those who seriously follow the process of Kṛṣṇa consciousness, though previously habituated to many undesirable things, are able to stay on a platform where there is no material contamination simply by virtue of practicing Kṛṣṇa consciousness.

Thus Kṛṣṇa consciousness is an excellent medicine. Unless one comes to awareness of Kṛṣṇa, the habits he forms in association with the three modes of material nature will continue, and he will not be able to change them. If one actually wants freedom from the repetition of birth and death, he must come to Kṛṣṇa consciousness. In *Bhagavad-gītā* Lord Kṛṣṇa says:

māṁ ca yo 'vyabhicāreṇa
bhakti-yogena sevate

sa guṇān samatītyaitān
brahma-bhūyāya kalpate

"One who engages in full devotional service, who does not fall down in any circumstance, at once transcends the modes of material nature and thus comes to the level of Brahman." (Bg. 14.26)

The Kṛṣṇa consciousness process does not recommend this atonement or that atonement. One can go on experimenting by atoning, but the diseases of the soul will remain unless one comes to the platform of rendering devotional service in love and purifying his life.

4/Learning Tapasya, Self-Control

If one does not come to Kṛṣṇa consciousness, he may be relieved for the time being from the reactions of sinful activities, but he will again commit transgressions. Therefore Parīkṣit Mahārāja said: *kvacin nivartate 'bhadrāt kvacic carati tat punaḥ prāyaścittam ato 'pārtham:* "Repetitive sinning and atoning seem to me like nothing but a waste of time." He gave the example of an elephant which cleanses his body thoroughly in a lake or reservoir, but as soon as he comes onto shore he takes dust and throws it all over his body and immediately becomes dirty again. Thus Parīkṣit Mahārāja said that although one may cleanse himself in the process of atonement, if he again commits the same sinful acts, what is the use? Therefore the second question put by Parīkṣit Mahārāja to Śukadeva Gosvāmī is very important: How can one ultimately become free from all contamination brought about by the material modes of nature? If one cannot achieve liberation, what is the use of atonement?

In answer, Śukadeva Gosvāmī said that merely counteracting *karma,* fruitive activities, by other activities cannot bring one's miseries to a final end. For example, the United Nations is attempting to establish peace in the world, but they cannot stop war. War breaks out again and again. After the First World War statesmen and diplomats manufactured the League of Nations. Then the Second World War came, and now they have devised the United Nations, but war is still going on. The actual goal is to stop war, but that cannot be done. By one action war is created, and by another action war is stopped for the time being, but again at the next opportunity there is another war. The cycle of sinful activities and atonement is like that. What we actually want is to be free from suffering and war, but that does not happen.

Śukadeva Gosvāmī said that one kind of war causes a disturbance, and another kind of war stops it for some time, but that is not the ultimate solution to the problem. Śukadeva states that these troubles happen due to ignorance: *avidvad-adhikāritvāt. Avidvat* means "lack of knowledge." *Avidvat-adhikāritvāt prāyaścittaṁ vimarśanam.* Real atonement is performed in knowledge. Why is there fighting and why are there miseries? Unless these "why" questions, which in the *Vedas* are called *Kena Upaniṣad,* arise in one's mind, one is not fulfilling the proper function of his human life. These questions must arise: "Why am I suffering? Wherefrom have I come? What is my constitutional position? Where shall I go after death? Why am I put into a miserable form of life? Why are there birth, death, old age and disease?"

How can these questions be solved? Śukadeva Gosvāmī says: *nāśnataḥ pathyam evānnaṁ vyādhayo 'bhibhavanti hi/ evaṁ niyamakṛd rājan śanaiḥ kṣemāya kalpate.* If one wants to actually stop diseased life, he must follow a regulative principle.

If a person does not follow the program given by a physician to cure his disease, he cannot be cured. Similarly, if one does not think or act wisely, as Vedic knowledge prescribes, how can he stop the problems of life? Simply by atonement there may be a temporary suppression of difficulties, but they will arise again.

Śukadeva Gosvāmī says that in material or sinful life we act in a way in which we are forced to commit sins and suffer as a result. This is so, and if we want to stop this cycle of suffering and victimization, we have to advance in knowledge. Ordinary people, or *karmīs,* are fruitive actors who work all day and night to get some enjoyable results and then again suffer. Thus the problems of such *karmīs* are never solved. It is suggested therefore that one elevate himself to the platform of knowledge as prescribed in *Śrīmad-Bhāgavatam.* The first necessity is *tapasya,* or acceptance of austerity. If a doctor advises a diabetic patient not to eat but to starve for some days, although no one likes to starve, the patient must voluntarily accept starvation if he wants to be cured. This is *tapasya:* voluntary acceptance of a miserable condition. The ability to do this is good, and human life is meant for that purpose. Indeed, Vedic culture prescribes *tapasya,* and one can see many *tapasvīs* undergoing austerities in India. In the winter they stand in water up to their necks and meditate. Standing in water during severe cold is not very comfortable, but they voluntarily do it. In the summer they also ignite fires all around themselves and sit down in the midst of the blazes and meditate. These are examples of severe *tapasya* undertaken by many ascetics in India.

Some *tapasya* is certainly required. Without it, one can not advance in spiritual life or knowledge. If we simply engage in the animal propensities of eating, sleeping, mating and defending, not accepting the *tapasya* process, human life is a failure. If one wants to become an initiated member of our Kṛṣṇa consciousness society, we first of all ask him to undergo *tapasya*. In the Western countries especially it is a great *tapasya* to give up illicit sex life, intoxication, meat-eating and gambling. Although we require only these austerities, it is very difficult to observe them. In England, a wealthy aristocrat inquired from a Vaiṣṇava Godbrother: "Svāmijī, can you make me a *brāhmaṇa*?" The Svāmijī replied, "Yes, why not? You just have to observe these four principles—no illicit sex, intoxication, gambling and meat-eating." "Impossible," the Britisher replied. Yes, it is impossible, for in Europe or in America self-indulgence is the way of life from the very beginning. Indian gentlemen often come to the West to learn these indulgences, and they think themselves to be thus advancing. Indians are automatically taught *tapasya* through their Vedic culture, but they come to America to forget that culture and accept another type of life. The real fact is, however, that if one wants to advance in spiritual understanding and solve all the problems of life, he must accept this life of *tapasya*—austerity and restriction.

Restriction is for human beings, not for animals. We encounter restrictions daily in our common dealings. We cannot drive a car on the left or run a red light without risking apprehension by the law. If a dog, however, walks on the left side of the street or crosses against a red light, it is not punished because it is an animal. The law therefore makes distinctions between human beings and animals because human beings supposedly have advanced consciousness. If we do not follow rules and regulations, we again lapse into animalism. Apparently propaganda is being made celebrating freedom as opposed to a regulated life, but one who sees things as they are can understand that freedom from all restriction is animal life. Therefore Śukadeva Gosvāmī recommends *tapasya.* If we want actual freedom from the problems of life, we have to accept a life of austerity. Bondage to material life is the only other alternative.

What is *tapasya*? What is austerity? The first principal of austerity is *brahmacarya,* restricted sex life. The real meaning of *brahmacarya* is complete celibacy, and according to Vedic culture in the beginning of life one should strictly follow the regulations of *brahmacarya.* When he is grown up, the *brahmacārī* can marry and become *gṛhastha,* and as a *gṛhastha* he can have sex, but in the *brahmacarya* life strict celibacy is the rule. In the present age people have become degraded for want of *tapasya* because they are not taught how to execute *tapasvī* life. Criticism for its own sake will not do; one must be effectively trained in the life of *tapasya.*

In the *Vedas* it is said that those who execute a regulated life of *tapasya* are *brāhmaṇas. Etad akṣaraṁ gārgi viditvāsmāl lokāt praiti sa brāhmaṇaḥ/ etad akṣaraṁ gārgy aviditvāsmāl lokāt praiti sa kṛpaṇaḥ.* Everyone is dying, for no one can live here permanently, but one who dies after executing a life of *tapasya* is a *brāhmaṇa,* and one who dies like a cat or dog, without executing *tapasya,* is called a *kṛpaṇa.* These two words are used frequently in Vedic literature—*brāhmaṇa* and *kṛpaṇa. Kṛpaṇa* means "miser" and *brāhmaṇa* refers to a liberal, broadminded person. *Brahma jānātīti brāhmaṇaḥ:* One who knows the supreme, the Absolute Truth, is a *brāhmaṇa,* but one who does not know is an animal. This is the difference between animal and man; man, to deserve the name, must be educated to understand the Absolute Truth. Because human life is meant for knowledge, there are schools and colleges, philosophers and scientists and mathematicians. The processes of eating, sleeping, mating and defending need not be taught, for they are learned instinctively. Human life is obviously meant for more. It is meant for *tapasya* and knowledge.

There are descriptions in the *Vedas* of *brahmacarya,* celibacy, which characterize the beginning of a life dedicated to *tapasya: Smaraṇaṁ kīrtanaṁ keliḥ prekṣaṇaṁ guhya-bhāṣaṇam/ saṅkalpo 'dhyavasāyaś ca kriyā-nirvṛttir eva ca* (Śrīdhara 6.1.12). To properly execute celibacy, one should not even think or even talk of sex life. Reading modern literatures and newspapers which are filled with sexual material is also against the principles of *brahmacarya.* Similarly, indulging in sex in any way, looking at and whispering with girls, and determining or endeavoring to engage in sex life are all against the principles of *brahmacarya.* One executes real *brahmacarya* when all these activities come to a halt.

By austerity, celibacy, and control of the mind and senses one can advance in pure life. Similarly, advancement can be made through charity properly directed. That is called *tyāga,* renunciation. If one has a million dollars, he should not keep it, but, as long as it is within his jurisdiction, he should spend it for Kṛṣṇa. Money or energy is properly utilized when it is directed to Kṛṣṇa.

As soon as one quits his body, all his monetary resources and everything else that he has collected in connection with his body is finished, for the spirit soul transmigrates to another body, and one does not know where the money which he earned in his previous body is being kept or how it is being spent. A person may leave the world declaring how the money should be spent by his sons or heirs, but even if one leaves millions of dollars, in his next life he has no claim to it. Therefore as long as it is in one's hand, it is better to spend it for a good purpose. If one spends it for bad purposes, he becomes entangled, but if he spends it for good purposes, he gets good in return. This is very clearly stated in *Bhagavad-gītā.*

Bhagavad-gītā explains that there are three kinds of charity—charity in the mode of goodness, passion and ignorance. A person in the mode of goodness knows where charity should be given. In *Bhagavad-gītā* Kṛṣṇa says:

samo 'haṁ sarva-bhūteṣu
na me dveṣyo 'sti na priyaḥ
ye bhajanti tu māṁ bhaktyā
mayi te teṣu cāpy aham

"I envy no one, nor am I partial to anyone. I am equal to all. But whoever renders service unto Me in devotion is a friend, is in Me, and I am also a friend to him." (Bg. 9.29)

Kṛṣṇa is not in want of money, for He is the original proprietor of everything *(Īśāvāsyam idaṁ sarvam)*. But still He asks us for charity. For example, Kṛṣṇa, in the guise of Vāmana, a dwarf *brāhmaṇa*, went to beg from Bali Mahārāja. Even though He is *sarva-loka-maheśvaram*, the proprietor of all the planets, He nonetheless says, "Please give in charity to Me." Why? It is for our interest, for the sooner we return Kṛṣṇa's money to Kṛṣṇa, the better situated we will be. Of course this may not be very pleasant to hear, but actually we are all thieves, for we have stolen God's property. If one who has something is not God conscious, it is to be understood that he has stolen God's property. That is the nature of material life. If this is considered thoughtfully and if one comes to real knowledge, he will realize that if we do not understand God, whose property we are using, whatever we possess is stolen property. It is also stated in *Bhagavad-gītā* that if one does not spend his money for *yajña,* sacrifice, he is understood to be a thief *(yo bhuṅkte stena eva saḥ).* For instance, if one earns a great deal of money but tries to hide it to avoid paying income tax, the government considers him to be a criminal. He cannot say, "I have earned this money. Why shall I pay tax to the government?" No, he must pay or risk punishment. Similarly, in the higher sense everything we have is Kṛṣṇa's or God's, and it must be utilized in accordance with His desires. We may wish to construct a building, but where do we get the stone, wood and earth that the construction requires? We cannot artificially produce the wood; it is God's property. We cannot produce the metal; we must take it from the mine, which is also God's property. The earth and the bricks which are made from it are also God's. We simply give our labor, but that labor is also God's property. We work with our hands, but they are not our hands but God's, for when the power to use the hand is withdrawn by God, the hand becomes useless.

We should use this great opportunity, human life, to understand all these points which are mentioned in the authoritative books of Vedic knowledge like *Śrīmad-Bhāgavatam* and *Bhagavad-gītā.* In the *Bhāgavatam* Śukadeva Gosvāmī declares that real atonement necessitates thoughtfulness, sobriety and meditation. One must consider whether he is the body or whether he is transcendental to the body, and one must try to know what God is. These ideas are to be studied in Kṛṣṇa consciousness. We should not be frivolous or waste time. If one wants this knowledge, he has to practice austerity, *tapasya,* and the beginning of *tapasya,* as already explained, is *brahmacarya*—celibacy or restricted sex life. The pivot of material attraction is sex, not only for human society but for animal society also. Sparrows and pigeons have sex three hundred times daily, although they are strict vegetarians, and the lion, which is not a vegetarian, has sex once a year. Spiritual life is not a question of vegetarianism but of understanding higher knowledge. When one comes to the platform of elevated knowledge, he naturally becomes a vegetarian. *Paṇḍitāḥ sama-darśinaḥ:* one who is very highly learned does not distinguish between a learned scholar, a *brāhmaṇa,* an elephant, a dog and a cow. He is *sama-darśī;* his vision enables him to see them all equally. How is this? He does not see the body but the soul, the spiritual spark (Brahman). He thinks: "Here is a dog, but it is also a living entity, although by his past *karma* he has become a dog. And this learned scholar is also a living spark, but he has taken good birth because of his past *karma.*" When one comes to that position, he does not see the body, but the spiritual spark, and he does not distinguish between one living entity and another.

Actually we do not make distinctions between carnivores and vegetarians, for the grass has life just as the cow or the lamb. A guideline, however, should be the Vedic instruction given in *Īśopaniṣad:*

īśāvāsyam idaṁ sarvaṁ
yat kiñca jagatyāṁ jagat
tena tyaktena bhuñjīthā
mā gṛdhaḥ kasya svid dhanam

"Everything animate or inanimate that is within the universe is controlled and owned by the Lord. One should therefore accept only those things necessary for himself, which are set aside as his quota, and one must not accept other things, knowing well to whom they belong." (*Īśopaniṣad, Mantra* 1)

Since everything is the property of the Supreme Lord, one can only enjoy what is allotted to him by the Lord, and one cannot touch another's property. According to Vedic life and according to all Vedic scriptures, a man should live on fruits and vegetables, for his teeth are made in such a way that these can be very easily eaten and digested. Although it is nature's law that one has to live by eating other living entities *(jīvo jīvasya jīvanam),* one must use discretion. Fruits, flowers, vegetables, rice, grain and milk are made for human beings. Milk, for example, is an animal product, the blood of an animal transformed, but the cow delivers more milk than is needed by her calf because milk is intended for man. Man should simply take the milk and let the cows live, and thus following nature's law, man will be happy. *Tena tyaktena bhuñjīthā:* one should take whatever God allots to him and thus live comfortably.

We have to elevate our consciousness through this science of Kṛṣṇa. Charity is within everyone's heart, but we do not know how to make the best use of it.

Whatever we spend in terms of energy should be for Kṛṣṇa, for it all belongs to Him. By spending for Kṛṣṇa, one will not be a loser. Kṛṣṇa is so kind that when we offer Him food, He accepts and yet leaves everything for us to eat. Simply by offering food to Kṛṣṇa we can become devotees. We need not spend an extra farthing. In the higher sense, everything belongs to Kṛṣṇa, but if we offer everything to Kṛṣṇa, we will be elevated. This is a sublime and proven way for advancement in pure life.

5/Learning Steadiness in Kṛṣṇa Consciousness

When one reaches the topmost position of material opulence, the tendency for renunciation is natural. There are two tendencies in this material world—*bhoga* (sense enjoyment) and *tyāga* (renunciation of this material world). Without guidance, however, one does not know how to renounce. First of all, one wants to enjoy, and when he is frustrated in enjoyment, he renounces. Again, when he is tired of renunciation, he enjoys, like a clock pendulum which swings from side to side. We are thus all vacillating from the platform of enjoyment to the platform of renunciation and back again.

Karmīs, fruitive workers, try to enjoy this world and reap the fruits of it. Consequently, they are constantly traveling on expressways all day and night to engage in material enjoyment. On the other hand, there are others, predominantly the discontented youth, who don't want any part of this. Thus the world contains those engaged in *bhoga* and those engaged in *tyāga.* However, we will not be happy by following either of these paths because it is not our proper position to either enjoy or renounce. Since everything belongs to Kṛṣṇa and nothing belongs to anyone else, whatever we possess is actually Kṛṣṇa's property (*īśāvāsyam idaṁ sarvam*). Since we have not produced the trees, plants, waters or the land, we cannot claim them. Since we actually have nothing, we can renounce nothing, or, as it is said, naked we come into this world and naked we go out. In the interim we falsely claim, "This is my country, this is my home, this is my wife, these are my children, this is my property, this is my bank balance, etc." Such claims are false because when we come into the world, we come in empty-handed, and when we go out, we go out empty-handed. What then is the meaning of *bhoga* and *tyāga?* In the light of the actual facts, they have no actual meaning. *Bhoga* is thievery, and *tyāga*, renunciation of what never belonged to us, is a form of lunacy.

In this regard, Kṛṣṇa gives us this direction: *sarva-dharmān parityajya mām ekaṁ śaraṇaṁ vraja.* (Bg. 18.66) Although we have created different types of religion based on *bhoga* and *tyāga,* we are thus advised to give up all of them and to surrender unto Kṛṣṇa. It is not within our power to enjoy or to renounce. When renunciation is recommended in *Bhagavad-gītā,* it refers to renunciation of everything that we falsely claim to possess. A child may take a hundred dollar bill from his father and try to keep it although he may not know how to use it. The father may beg the child, "Dear boy, kindly give it to me." The child does not know that the money actually belongs to the father, nor does he know that he had best hand it to his father, for he simply does not know how to use it. Similarly, Kṛṣṇa says, "Renounce your work for Me. Renounce your wealth and property for Me." Kṛṣṇa is not a beggar, for everything belongs to Him, but He does treat us like small children. Compliance to His request to give everything to Him is called *tyāga*, renunciation, and is one of the means by which one can attain elevation to Kṛṣṇa consciousness. Austerity, celibacy, equanimity and charity are all required for realization of the ultimate or Absolute Truth. Kṛṣṇa consciousness is not concerned with the relative truth but with the Absolute. In *Śrīmad-Bhāgavatam* Vyāsadeva offers his obeisances to the Supreme Absolute Truth (*satyaṁ paraṁ dhīmahi*). He offers his respects not to the relative categorical truths, but to the *summum bonum,* the Absolute Truth. It is the duty of *brāhmaṇas* to practice those qualities by which the Absolute Truth can be realized.

Brāhmaṇas must be qualified by practicing cleanliness, truthfulness, control of the mind and the senses, simplicity, and by cultivating faith in the *Vedas* and particularly in *Bhagavad-gītā.* When Kṛṣṇa says, "I am the Supreme Lord," we have to accept Him with faith, not foolishly, but with full knowledge, and practically apply this acceptance in our daily life. A *brāhmaṇa* is not created by birth, but by education, practice and knowledge. It is not a question of birth, but quality, as pointed out by Kṛṣṇa in *Bhagavad-gītā:*

cātur-varṇyaṁ mayā sṛṣṭaṁ
guṇa-karma-vibhāgaśaḥ
tasya kartāram api māṁ
viddhy akartāram avyayam

"According to the three modes of material nature and the work ascribed to them, the four divisions of human society were created by Me. And, although I am the creator of this system, you should know that I am yet the non-doer, being unchangeable." (Bg. 4.13)

One must not only have the qualities of a *brāhmaṇa,* but one should also work as a *brāhmaṇa,* for one's qualities are tested by his work. If one is a qualified engineer but simply sits down at home and does not work, what is his value? Similarly, unless one works as a *brāhmaṇa,* there is no value to his simply saying, "I am a *brāhmaṇa.*" One must therefore work as a *brāhmaṇa* by fully engaging in the service of Param Brahman, Kṛṣṇa, the Supreme Brahman.

How can service to the Absolute Truth be executed? *Yamena niyamena ca:* the practice of *yoga,* or linking with the supreme, is based on the principles of regulation and control. Regulation cannot be executed without control; therefore one must be thoughtful and purify himself. If one wants to pass an examination, he has to go to school, follow the principles of the school, and take some pains in his study, and then gradually he comes to be successful. If he plays all day on the street, how can he expect success? Therefore in the process being explained by Śukadeva Gosvāmī, the first necessity is *tapasya,* austerity. Even if austerity and *brahmacarya* are painful because we want to be unrestricted, as soon as we are regulated, what appeared to be painful is in practice not painful.

There are two classes of men—those who are sober (*dhīra*) and those who are extravagant (*adhīra*).

When one, in spite of provocation or in spite of the presence of a source of mental agitation, can remain steady in his position, he is called *dhīra.* An example of a *dhīra* is given by Kālidāsa Paṇḍita, a great Sanskrit poet who wrote a book called *Kumāra-sambhava,* wherein he has given an example concerning Lord Śiva. It appears that when the demigods were fighting the demons and were being defeated, they decided that they could be saved by a commander-in-chief born from the semina of Lord Śiva. Lord Śiva, however, was in meditation, and to acquire the needed semina was very difficult. They therefore sent Pārvatī, a young girl, who appeared before Lord Śiva and worshiped his genitals. Although this young girl sat before Lord Śiva and touched his genitals, Lord Śiva was steady in meditation. Kālidāsa says, "Here is an example of a *dhīra,* for despite a young girl's touching his genitals, he was undisturbed."

Similarly, someone sent a young prostitute to disturb Haridāsa Ṭhākura, and upon hearing her appeals for intercourse, Haridāsa Ṭhākura said, "Yes, your proposal is very nice. Please sit down and let me finish my chanting, and then we shall enjoy." Morning came and the prostitute became impatient, but Haridāsa Ṭhākura replied, "I'm very sorry. I could not finish my chanting. Come tonight again." The prostitute came for three nights, and on the third night she fell down at his feet, confessed her intentions, and pleaded with him, "I was induced to perform this act by a man who is your enemy. Kindly excuse me." Haridāsa Ṭhākura then replied, "I know all about that, but I allowed you to come here for three days so that you could be converted and become a devotee. Now take these chanting beads, and go on chanting. I am leaving this place." Here is another example of a *dhīra* who has control of his body (*deha*), words (*vāc*), and intelligence (*buddhi*). One's body, words and intelligence should be controlled by one who is *dhīra* and who actually knows the principles of religion.

We have been continuously committing sinful activities since time immemorial, and we do not know when this began, but this life is meant for rectification of all the mistakes that we have committed. If one sets fire to unwanted grass and creepers in a field, they will all be burned. Similarly, by the process of austerity and penance, one can liquidate all sinful activities and become purified. But Śukadeva Gosvāmī suggests an alternate process: *kecit kevalayā bhaktyā vāsudeva-parāyaṇāḥ/ aghaṁ dhunvanti kārtsnyena nīhāram iva bhāskaraḥ*. Generally, if one leads an austere and pious life of celibacy, equanimity, charity, etc., people will say that he is a very pious man, but simply by becoming Kṛṣṇa conscious, one can kill all the resultant actions of his past sinful life. A fog disappears as soon as the sun rises, and Kṛṣṇa rises with the brilliance of thousands of suns.

This process is accepted only by someone who is very fortunate. Caitanya Mahāprabhu therefore said: *(eirūpa) brahmāṇḍa bhramite kona bhāgyavān jīva/ guru-kṛṣṇa-prasāde pāya bhakti-latā-bīja:* "By the grace of Kṛṣṇa and the spiritual master, a fortunate person, after wandering throughout the universe in different species of life, receives the seed of pure devotional service." Kṛṣṇa consciousness is meant for the very fortunate, for simply by accepting this one process a person can surpass all the duties of austerity, renunciation, celibacy, etc. Śukadeva Gosvāmī declares: *kecit kevalayā bhaktyā:* "One who is extremely fortunate takes to the process of pure devotional service." *Kevalā bhakti* refers to pure unalloyed devotional service in which there is no desire but to please Kṛṣṇa. One should not render devotional service just to increase his income. We want money to become happy, but if we take to Kṛṣṇa consciousness, automatically we will become so happy that we will neglect money. Money will automatically come. Happiness will come. There is no need to endeavor for these things separately.

It was Dhruva Mahārāja who lamented, "How foolish I was that I took to devotional service with a desire for material profit." Ordinarily for material profit one goes to his boss or some rich man or demigod, but a devotee does not go anywhere but to Kṛṣṇa, even if he has material desires. If one goes to Kṛṣṇa even for material advantages, the day will come when he forgets material desires, just like Dhruva Mahārāja. He was repentant, and said, "I came to Kṛṣṇa and asked for something material, just like one who has pleased a very rich man and who asks him for a few grains of rice." If a rich man agrees to give us whatever we want, but we ask him only for a few grains of rice, is that very intelligent? Asking Kṛṣṇa for material benefit is exactly like this. One need not ask Kṛṣṇa extraneously for material happiness, for material happiness will automatically roll before his very feet, pleading, "Please take me, please take me."

Those who are practicing Kṛṣṇa consciousness are not in need of the material opulences—wives, children, happiness, home—for all is acquired automatically by the grace of Kṛṣṇa. There is no need to ask Kṛṣṇa for these material things, but one should simply request Him: "Please engage me in Your service." In *Bhagavad-gītā* Kṛṣṇa also promises that if one engages in His service, He will supply what is needed and preserve whatever is already possessed. One of His final instructions to Arjuna indicates total dependence on Him:

cetasā sarva-karmāṇi
mayi sannyasya mat-paraḥ
buddhi-yogam upāśritya
mac-cittaḥ satataṁ bhava

"In all activities, and for their results, just depend upon Me, and work always under My protection. In such devotional service, be fully conscious of Me." (Bg. 18.57)

6/Transcending Designations and Problems

Kṛṣṇa consciousness is easily achieved by the mercy of Lord Caitanya, but only some are fortunate enough to have the mercy of Lord Caitanya and His disciplic succession. According to *Bhagavad-gītā:*

manuṣyāṇāṁ sahasreṣu
kaścid yatati siddhaye
yatatām api siddhānāṁ
kaścin māṁ vetti tattvataḥ

"Out of many thousands among men, one may endeavor for perfection, and of those who have achieved perfection, hardly one knows Me in truth." (Bg. 7.3)

God realization is not possible for animals or for persons who are almost animals, or for animals in the shape of human beings. Contemporary civilization is by in large an assembly of animals because, as stated before, it operates on the basis of the animal propensities. The birds and beasts arise early in the morning and busy themselves trying to find food and sex and trying to defend themselves; at night they look for shelter, and in the morning they fly to a tree to find nuts and fruits. Similarly, in New York City, great hordes of people travel from one island to another by ferry boat or wait for subways in order to go to the office for the purpose of finding food. How is this an advancement over animal life? Although the ferry and subway are always crowded, and many people have to travel forty or fifty miles for bread, the birds are free to fly from one tree to another.

Real civilization is not concerned simply with man's animal needs but with enabling man to understand his relationship with God, the supreme father. One may learn about his relationship with God by any process—through Christianity, through the Vedic literatures or through the *Koran*—but in any case it must be learned. The purpose of this Kṛṣṇa consciousness movement is not to make Christians into Hindus or Hindus into Christians but to inform everyone that the duty of a human being is to understand his relationship with God. One must learn this, otherwise he is simply wasting his time by engaging in animalistic propensities. We must all try to love Kṛṣṇa or God. If one has a process, he should practice it, or he can come and learn this process. One should not begrudge the selection of one process over another. *Viṣād apy amṛtaṁ grāhyam amedhyād api kāñcanam/ nīcād apy uttamāṁ vidyāṁ strī-ratnaṁ duṣkulād api* (*Nīti-darpaṇa* 1.16). Cāṇakya Paṇḍita says that one must catch what is right from any source. If there is a glass of poison with some nectar in it, he says, one should take out the nectar and leave the poison. In the same way, if one finds gold in a filthy place, he should take it. Similarly, although according to the Vedic system of education one must be given instruction by intellectual persons like *brāhmaṇas,* if someone lower on the social scale has learned the truth, one should accept him as a teacher and learn from him. One should not think that just because one is lowly born he should not be accepted as a teacher.

Similarly, if one is serious about understanding God, he should not think, "I am Christian," "I am Hindu," or "I am Muslim." If one is serious about understanding love of God, he should consider which process is practical. One should not think, "Why should I follow Hindu or Vedic scriptures?" The purpose of following the Vedic scriptures is to develop love of God. When students come to America for a higher education, they do not consider the fact that the teachers may be American, German or of other nationalities. If one wants a higher education, he simply comes and takes it. Similarly, if there is an effective process for understanding and approaching God, like this Kṛṣṇa consciousness process, one should take it.

Not all, but those who are intelligent and fortunate take to this process of devotional service *(kevalayā bhaktyā)*, and their only desire is to serve Kṛṣṇa. From early morning till late at night the devotees are engaged in Kṛṣṇa's service. This is called *kevalayā*, pure; for them there is no other business. This process is recommended for all, and it is the perfection of all religious processes. *(Sa vai puṁsāṁ paro dharmo yato bhaktir adhokṣaje).* In Sanskrit, there are two words, *para,* and *apara,* which describe the superior (transcendental) and the inferior (material) approaches to religion. In the execution of material *dharma,* or religion performed for material gain, people generally go to a church or a temple and pray, "God, give us our daily bread." Actually, this need not be asked for, for bread is already provided for everyone. Even the birds and beasts get their bread without having to go to church to ask God for it. Similarly, our bread is also provided, whether we go to church or not. That is not a problem, for no one is dying in the streets of starvation, nor do we find a bird, beast, or even an ant dying of starvation. Food is there, and one need not bother about it. If the brain should be taxed, it should be taxed for Kṛṣṇa or God. This is the proper utilization of time. There is no scarcity of bread in the Kingdom of God.

Tasyaiva hetoḥ prayateta kovido na labhyate yad bhramatām uparyadhaḥ. Śrīmad-Bhāgavatam says that one should try to attain that which cannot be attained by traveling all over the universe. What is that? *Kevalayā bhaktyā*—pure devotion. By God's arrangement there is sufficient food, land and prospects for food on this planet, but we have arranged things in such a way that in one part of the world people are suffering and in another part they are throwing grains in the ocean. The *Vedas* say, *eko bahūnāṁ yo vidadhāti kāmān*—the Supreme Person is supplying food to many living entities. The difficulty in this material world is that we take more than we need and thus create our own problems. Problems are created by men, led by the so-called politicians. According to nature's way or God's way, everything is complete. According to *Śrī Īśopaniṣad:*

oṁ pūrṇam adaḥ pūrṇam idaṁ
pūrṇāt pūrṇam udacyate
pūrṇasya pūrṇam ādāya
pūrṇam evāvaśiṣyate

"The Personality of Godhead is perfect and complete, and because of this all emanations from Him, such as this phenomenal world, are perfectly equipped as complete wholes. Whatever is produced of the complete whole is also complete in itself. Because He is the complete whole, even though so many complete units emanate from Him, He remains the complete balance." (*Śrī Īśopaniṣad,* Invocation) God is complete, His creation is complete, and His arrangements are complete, but we are creating disturbances. Real education is that which makes people Kṛṣṇa conscious so that they will properly utilize the resources of the earth and stop creating disturbances. It is not possible to solve problems by passing resolutions in the United Nations. One must know the actual method of solving problems.

Śukadeva Gosvāmī says that simply by pure devotional service one can solve the problems of life. Who can do this? It is not possible for an ordinary man but for those who are *vāsudeva-parāyaṇāḥ*, devoted to Lord Kṛṣṇa (Vāsudeva). Only those whose concern is to satisfy Kṛṣṇa and who take to pure unalloyed devotional service can solve the problems of life.

Aghaṁ dhunvanti—as already explained, problems are created by sinful activities. Although there is enough food, everyone stocks more than is needed in order to make a profit or simply in order to hoard. In 1942, in India, there was an artificial famine created by people gathering money and stocking it unnecessarily. Wealthy men collected rice which was selling at six rupies a pound, and suddenly within a week the price rose to fifty rupies a pound. Consequently no rice was available on the market, and the people went hungry. An American gentleman present at the time remarked, "If people in our country were starving in this way, there would have been a revolution." The people in India, however, are so trained and cultured that in spite of this artificial famine they did not revolt but preferred to die peacefully. Of course, this is only one instance, but it shows how problems are not created by God but by man. In Germany during the First World War the women went to church and prayed to God to send their husbands, sons and brothers back safely, but none of them came back. All of the women became atheists. They did not consider that God did not advocate the war and its problems. They went to Him for a solution. When we create our own problems, we have to suffer the results.

It is a fact, however, that the problems of one who takes to the shelter of Kṛṣṇa, God, are solved. For this reason, if for none other, one should apply his devotional service to Vāsudeva, the Supreme Personality of Godhead. *Vāsudeve bhagavati bhakti-yogaḥ prayojitaḥ.* If one engages in devotional service to Vāsudeva, he will receive the highest knowledge without delay *(janayaty āśu vairāgyam).* The words *jñāna-vairāgyam* refer to "that knowledge by which one becomes detached from material allurement." The word *jñāna* means knowledge, and *vairāgyam* means detachment. Both knowledge and detachment are required in this human form of life. One should know: "I am spirit soul. I have nothing to do with this material world, but because I have a desire to enjoy it in different ways, I am transmigrating from one body to another. I do not know when this began, but it is still going on." This is real knowledge. To be knowledgeable, one must understand his constitutional position and realize how he is suffering in this material world. That perfection of knowledge comes when one becomes *Vāsudeva-parāyaṇāḥ,* devoted to Lord Vāsudeva. In *Bhagavad-gītā,* Lord Kṛṣṇa tells Arjuna:

bahūnāṁ janmanām ante
jñānavān māṁ prapadyate
vāsudevaḥ sarvam iti
sa mahātmā sudurlabhaḥ

"After many births and deaths, he who is actually in knowledge surrenders unto Me, knowing Me to be the cause of all causes and all that is. Such a great soul is very rare." (Bg. 7.19) Those great souls who know perfectly well that Kṛṣṇa, Vāsudeva, is the source of everything, are very rare. It is easy to find so-called *mahātmās* (great souls) with long beards and mustaches who tell everyone that they are one with God and that when they die they will wake up and become God, but these are not really *mahātmās.* Rather, they are *durātmā,* hard-hearted, because they want to encroach on the rightful position of

Kṛṣṇa and become one with Him. If there were a servant in the office who tried to occupy the position of employer, would the employer like it? Similarly, any living entity who is trying to become God is not very much to God's liking. Of course no one can become God, but this endeavor to become God or His competitor is not very pleasing to Him. Persons who try are described in *Bhagavad-gītā* as *dviṣataḥ,* envious. The Lord says:

tān ahaṁ dviṣataḥ krūrān
saṁsāreṣu narādhamān
kṣipāmy ajasram aśubhān
āsurīṣv eva yoniṣu

"Envious, mischievous, the lowest of mankind, these do I ever put back into the ocean of material existence, into various demoniac species of life." (Bg. 16.19)

They are put into hellish conditions because they are envious of God's position. First they try to occupy high positions in this material world, and when they are frustrated in this attempt, they think, "Now I shall occupy the position of God." Of course this desire is also frustrated because no one can become God. God is God, and the living entity is the living entity. God is supreme and infinite; we are infinitesimal. Our position is to serve God, and when we act according to our position, we become happy. By imitating God, happiness cannot be obtained. *Yasyaika-niśvasita-kālam athāvalambya jīvanti loma-*

vilajā jagad-aṇḍa-nāthāḥ. (Bs. 5.48) There are innumerable universes, and within one breath of the Mahā-Viṣṇu these universes are inhaled and dissolved within His body. How then can a living entity become God? God is not so cheap. Therefore we must become advanced in knowledge and accept Vāsudeva, Kṛṣṇa, as the supreme. There is no question of Kṛṣṇa being a man. At no stage in His appearance on earth did He appear as an ordinary living entity. Even as a baby He performed miraculous feats way beyond the abilities of the ordinary living entity. One should not consider that when he is surrendering to Kṛṣṇa he is surrendering to an ordinary man but to the Supreme Personality of Godhead. Indeed, that is confirmed by all Vedic literatures. *Aghaṁ dhunvanti:* All reactions to sinful activities are cancelled when one surrenders to Kṛṣṇa. In *Bhagavad-gītā* Lord Kṛṣṇa Himself advises personal surrender to Him:

sarva-dharmān parityajya
mām ekaṁ śaraṇaṁ vraja
ahaṁ tvāṁ sarva-pāpebhyo
mokṣayiṣyāmi mā śucaḥ

"Give up all varieties of religiousness and just surrender unto Me, and in return I shall protect you from all sinful reactions. Therefore you have nothing to fear." (Bg. 18.66)

Therefore one who is a devotee *(Vāsudeva-parāyaṇāḥ)* and who simply engages in devotional service is immediately freed from all sinful activities. Devotional service to Kṛṣṇa or Kṛṣṇa consciousness can never be attained by any amount of speculation but by the causeless mercy of a pure devotee of Kṛṣṇa. It is a matchless gift bestowed by the *mahātmā* or great soul out of compassion for fallen living entities. It is said that by the grace of Kṛṣṇa one gets a *guru,* or a spiritual master, and by the grace of the spiritual master, one gets Kṛṣṇa. This is like the gift of the sunrise. At night there is darkness, but in the morning, as soon as the sun rises, immediately millions of miles of darkness are removed. In the same way, if we try to make the sun of Kṛṣṇa rise within our hearts, all of our problems will be solved.

7/The Matchless Gift: Liberation in Kṛṣṇa Consciousness

If we simply worship the original person (*ādi-puruṣam*), we need not fear being misled by anyone. Śrīdhara Svāmī, the original commentator on *Śrīmad-Bhāgavatam*, explains that one can reach the perfection of life simply by devotional service (*kevalayā bhaktyā*); one need not be dependent on any other process. Śukadeva Gosvāmī says that one can put an end to material life by one stroke (*kevalayā*). There is no need to first undergo severe penance and austerity, practice celibacy, control the mind and the senses, give in charity, perform great sacrifices and become very truthful and clean. Simply by one stroke—by accepting Kṛṣṇa consciousness—one immediately rises to the highest position. By just taking to Kṛṣṇa consciousness, one develops all transcendental qualifications. The goldsmith uses a small hammer and taps the gold many times, but the blacksmith uses a large hammer and with one stroke his job is finished. This is the blacksmith's method: we take the big hammer of *bhakti-yoga* and finish all material life. There is no need to undergo the many lesser disciplines, nor to follow any other process. In actuality, there is no possibility of even following the other Vedic processes to perfection. For instance, the *haṭha-yoga* process would say: "You have to become a strict *brahmacārī* and sit in the forest with your body at a right angle to the ground, pressing your nose with your finger for six months." Who could follow such an instruction? Since such a method is not practical in this present age, the goldsmith method has to be discarded. The solution is to take the blacksmith's hammer of Kṛṣṇa consciousness and finish off all sinful reactions immediately.

By devotional service one has to become *vāsudeva-parāyaṇa,* a devotee of Lord Vāsudeva or Lord Kṛṣṇa. In other words, we have to learn how to become lovers of Vāsudeva. If the world takes up this Kṛṣṇa consciousness, the planet is certain to be peaceful. Now the earth is quickly becoming a hellish planet, and if this Kṛṣṇa consciousness is not taken up, this hellish condition will progress despite all advances in education and economic development. Therefore those who are thoughtful should take this movement very seriously and try to understand its value. It is not something manufactured by one man or a group of disciples. It is authoritative and age-old, based on the Vedic literatures which date back thousands of years.

Nīhāram iva bhāskaraḥ. Bhāskara refers to the sun. The sun immediately dissipates mist or fog as well as darkness. As stated before, we should try to make the sun of Kṛṣṇa rise within our hearts. In the *Caitanya-caritāmṛta* also it is stated that Kṛṣṇa is like the sun and that *māyā,* the illusory energy, is darkness. *Yāhāṅ kṛṣṇa, tāhāṅ nāhi māyāra adhikāra:* As soon as the sun of Kṛṣṇa is present, the darkness of *māyā* immediately disappears. Without following this process, it is very difficult to overcome the ocean of darkness, *māyā.* If we simply teach people to surrender unto Kṛṣṇa, God, all the fog and mist of illusion will disappear. The method is very simple: chant Hare Kṛṣṇa, Hare Kṛṣṇa, Kṛṣṇa Kṛṣṇa, Hare Hare/ Hare Rāma, Hare Rāma, Rāma Rāma, Hare Hare.

The more one goes on chanting, the more the darkness of many lives is dissipated. *Ceto-darpaṇa-mārjanam:* by chanting, one can cleanse the dust from the mirror of his mind and perceive things very distinctly. Thus one will know what he is, what God is, what this world is, what our relationship with God in this world is, how to live in this world, and what our next life is. Such knowledge is not taught in schools, where one is taught how to manufacture or acquire products for sense gratification. There is always a hard struggle going on involving man's attempt to dominate material nature. However, for every convenience he manages to produce, there is an inconvenience accompanying it. For example, recently some engineers designed an airplane which can fly at great speeds without danger. When the plane flies, however, it breaks windows all over the city. Our time is thus being wasted in constructing so many devices which give us temporary and artificial convenience at the price of a proportionate amount of inconvenience. This is all part of the law of *karma*, the law of action and reaction. For whatever we do, there must be a reaction by which we become entangled. That is stated in *Bhagavad-gītā:*

yajñārthāt karmaṇo 'nyatra
loko 'yaṁ karma-bandhanaḥ
tad-arthaṁ karma kaunteya
mukta-saṅgaḥ samācara

"Work done as a sacrifice for Viṣṇu has to be performed, otherwise work binds one to this material world. Therefore, O son of Kuntī, perform your prescribed duties for His satisfaction, and in that way you will always remain unattached and free from bondage." (Bg. 3.9)

When one acts for sense gratification, work entangles him, whether the work be good or bad, but if one works for Kṛṣṇa *(yajnārthāt karmaṇo),* he will be free, regardless of the possible desirability of his work.

Not only does Śukadeva Gosvāmī recommend unalloyed devotional service, but he further says that by devotional service one's sinful activities will be negated. Every one of us is more or less sinful, for if we were not sinful we would not have been put into material bodies. As soon as one is free from sinful life, he is liberated and transferred to the spiritual world in a spiritual body. The whole process is to cleanse oneself from the contamination of sinful or material life.

Śukadeva Gosvāmī said, "My dear king, those who are sinful can become purified from contamination by *tapa-ādibhiḥ,* practicing austerity." Śukadeva also said, however, that no one can become completely purified by executing this process of austerity. There are many examples of *yogīs* who practiced austerities but did not emerge completely pure. Viśvāmitra Muni, for example, was a *kṣatriya* who wanted to become a *brāhmaṇa* and therefore began to practice austerity. Later on, however, he became a victim of Menakā, a society girl of the heavenly planets. Because Viśvāmitra was not pure, he became entangled with her and begot a child. Therefore it is said that even if one performs austerities and penances, worldly circumstances are so implicating that somehow or other they will involve one again and again in the material modes of nature. There are many examples of *sannyāsīs* who give up the world, renouncing it as false, saying, "Let me turn to Brahman," but they again become entangled in the work of the world when they set up hospitals and perform philanthropic work and welfare activities. If the world is false, why are they attracted to welfare activities? The philosophy of Kṛṣṇa consciousness maintains that this world is not false but that it is temporary. God created this world, and He is true, so how can His creation be false? Because this is the creation of God, and God is the Absolute Truth, this creation is also true. We simply see it otherwise due to illusion. The world is a fact, but it is a temporary fact.

A person may claim something within this world to be his property, but that is a false claim. It is a fact that it is someone's property, but it is God's property *(īśāvāsyam idaṁ sarvam).* This does not mean, however, that the property is false. What is false is the claim to the property, which is based upon a puffed up false consciousness that the individual is the proprietor, the master, or God. Everyone desires to be master or proprietor of something, then minister, then president, and then God. When everything else fails, the living entity wants to become God. The tendency is there to want to become the greatest of all, but the fact remains that God is the greatest and the living entity is small compared to Him. The smallest is not false, and the greatest is not false, but when the small thinks that he is great, that is false.

We understand from Vedic literature that Brahman, or the spirit, is *aṇor aṇīyāṁsam,* smaller than an atom, and *mahato mahīyāṁsam,* greater than the greatest. As far as we can conceive, the space which contains the universe is the greatest, but Kṛṣṇa has shown millions of universes in His mouth. The greatness of God cannot be comprehended by the living entities, who are part and parcel of God. As living entities, we are very minute, infinitesimal, and God is infinite. Indeed, the magnitude of the individual spirit soul is so microscopic that it cannot be seen. One cannot even imagine it with his material senses. Therefore it is said that the spirit soul is smaller than an atom *(aṇor aṇīyāṁsam).*

Since the living entities and Kṛṣṇa, the Supreme Lord, are both spirit, they are qualitatively one. Quantitatively, however, the Lord is great and the living entities are small. This fact can be accepted immediately on the basis of Vedic information. In *Brahma-saṁhitā* it is stated, *yasyaika-niśvasita-kālam athāvalambya jīvanti loma-vilajā jagad-aṇḍa-nāthāḥ:* many millions of universes come out of God's body when He exhales, and they again disappear when He inhales. Simply by His breathing, millions of universes are created and dissolved. If this is the case, then how can the living entities claim proprietorship over anything? One's position is safe only in so far as he does not falsely declare himself to be God or proprietor. It has become fashionable to claim to be God, and fools accept such claims, but from the Vedic literatures we understand that God is not so cheap.

As long as we are not making puffed up ego-centered claims, we are already liberated. There is no need to actually seek liberation. But as long as one thinks, "I am this body," he is not liberated. Liberation means knowing perfectly well that one's self is separate from the body. Therefore Śukadeva Gosvāmī said, *prāyaścittaṁ vimarśanam:* "Develop your knowledge; that will give you relief." Our knowledge is perfect when we come to know that we are very small particles of spiritual sparks, and that God, the supreme, the greatest spiritual identity, supplies all our necessities *(eko bahūnāṁ yo vidadhāti kāmān).* By knowing ourselves as minute particles, part and parcel of God, we can understand that our duty is to serve God. God is the center of all creation, of the whole universal body; He is the enjoyer, and we are His servitors. As this conception becomes clear, we become liberated.

Liberation entails freedom from all false conceptions. It is not that upon liberation one acquires ten hands. In *Śrīmad-Bhāgavatam* liberation is defined as *muktir hitvānyathā-rūpam. Mukti* means "to give up," and *anyathā-rūpam* denotes a false conception of life. This is to say that when one is situated in his original constitutional position, having given up all false notions, he is liberated. It is also said in *Śrīmad-Bhāgavatam* that by the aquisition of knowledge, one becomes liberated immediately. That knowledge can be very easily acquired, for it is simple: God is great, and I am very small; He is the supreme proprietor supplying all necessities, and I am His servant. Who can challenge this? It is a fact. We are simply under the false impression that we are this or that, and this leads us to the ultimate false impression that we are God. Yet we do not consider what manner of God we are. A small bodily disorder will send us to the physician. One who claims to be the supreme, therefore, should be understood to have fallen to the last snare of *māyā*. One who is thus fallen cannot even be liberated, for he is bound by false impressions.

Only when one has attained proper knowledge can he actually be liberated. The stage of liberation is also called the *brahma-bhūtaḥ* stage. One who has attained this stage is characterized by Śrī Kṛṣṇa in *Bhagavad-gītā* in this way:

brahma-bhūtaḥ prasannātmā
na śocati na kāṅkṣati
samaḥ sarveṣu bhūteṣu
mad-bhaktiṁ labhate parām

"One who is thus transcendentally situated at once realizes the Supreme Brahman. He never laments, or desires to have anything; he is equally disposed to every living entity. And in that state he achieves pure devotional service unto Me." (Bg. 18.54)

The joy which follows realization arises from understanding, "I was illusioned by false notions for so long. What a fool I was! I was thinking that I was God, but now I can understand that I am God's eternal servant." Upon gaining such realization, one attains liberation and becomes *prasannātmā,* or jolly, for this is the constitutional position of the living entity.

There is no lamentation when one is in pure consciousness, for he knows that he is a small part, a spiritual spark protected by the Supreme Lord. Where then is there scope for lamentation? A small child feels free as long as he knows that his father is there. He thinks, "My father is standing by me, so I am free. No one can harm me." Similarly, when one surrenders to Kṛṣṇa, he has complete faith that he is not in danger because Kṛṣṇa is protecting him. One who is thus surrendered to Kṛṣṇa is not subject to lamentation or desire, whereas one who is not God conscious simply hankers and laments. He hankers for that which he does not possess, and he laments for that which he did possess but has lost. A God conscious person is not subject to such misery. If something is lost, he knows that it is God's wish, and he thinks, "God desired this, so it is all right." He does not desire anything, for he knows that all his necessities are being provided by Kṛṣṇa, the supreme father.

As soon as one understands his relationship to God, he realizes universal brotherhood, for he understands that all men and animals—indeed, all life itself—are all parts of the supreme whole and are therefore all equal. Seeing this, one does not envy, exploit or trouble another living entity. Thus one who is a devotee of Kṛṣṇa automatically develops all good qualities, for he is in the proper consciousness. *Harāv abhaktasya kuto mahad-guṇā mano-rathenāsati dhāvato bahiḥ.* One who has developed Kṛṣṇa consciousness will manifest all the good qualities of the demigods. Indeed, it is stated, *vāñcā-kalpa-tarubhyaś ca kṛpā-sindhubhya eva ca:* A Vaiṣṇava or devotee of Kṛṣṇa is an ocean of mercy to others. He gives the greatest gift to society, for society is in dire need of God consciousness. A Vaiṣṇava bestows the priceless gift of the *mahāmantra,* Hare Kṛṣṇa, Hare Kṛṣṇa, Kṛṣṇa Kṛṣṇa, Hare Hare/ Hare Rāma, Hare Rāma, Rāma Rāma, Hare Hare. Simply by chanting this *mantra,* one can remain in a liberated state.

One should not think, however, that this state is simply a state of trance whereby one remains seated in lotus position in a corner for days on end. No, liberation means serving. One cannot simply say, "Now I have dedicated my life to Kṛṣṇa. Let me remain seated in *samādhi.*" The standard of surrender must be maintained by *niṣevayā,* serving. As one serves the Supreme Lord, the Lord reveals Himself within the heart. The program of devotional service to the Lord is executed from morning to night. Indeed, Kṛṣṇa says in *Bhagavad-gītā* that one must engage in devotional service to Him twenty-four hours a day. It is not that we should meditate for fifteen minutes and then engage in all kinds of nonsense. The more we serve, the more dedicated to Kṛṣṇa we become; therefore a person should utilize whatever talents he has for Kṛṣṇa. There are nine processes of devotional service—hearing, chanting, remembering, serving, worshiping the Deity in the temple, praying, carrying out orders, serving the Lord as friend, and sacrificing everything for Him—and one should always keep engaged in at least one of these nine processes. One who is always engaged in Kṛṣṇa's service never becomes disgusted *(bhajatāṁ prīti-pūrvakam).* Service must be rendered with love, but in the beginning this may be difficult, and so one may become disgusted. As one makes progress in Kṛṣṇa's service, however, he will find it pleasing. This is indicated by Kṛṣṇa in *Bhagavad-gītā:*

yat tad agre viṣam iva
pariṇāme 'mṛtopamam
tat sukhaṁ sāttvikaṁ proktam
ātma-buddhi-prasāda-jam

"That which in the beginning may be just like poison, but at the end is like nectar, and which awakens one to self-realization, is said to be happiness in the mode of goodness." (Bg. 18.37)

Once one has attained the spiritual platform, it is material service that actually becomes disgusting. For example, if one chants Hare Kṛṣṇa throughout his life, he will not grow tired of the names, but if one chants a material name over and over, he will soon become disgusted. The more one chants the names of Kṛṣṇa, the more he becomes attached. Thus service by *śravaṇam* and *kīrtanam,* hearing and chanting about Kṛṣṇa, is the beginning. The next process is *smaraṇam*—always remembering Kṛṣṇa. When one is perfect in chanting and hearing, he will always remember Kṛṣṇa. In this third stage, he becomes the greatest *yogī.*

Nor is progress in Kṛṣṇa consciousness ever lost. In the material world, if one begins to construct a factory but does not complete it, the factory is useless for all intents and purposes. If the construction is stopped and the building half finished, whatever money is invested is lost. This is not the case with Kṛṣṇa consciousness, for even if one does not come to the perfectional point, whatever work he does is his permanent asset, and he can begin from that point in his next life. Kṛṣṇa also confirms in *Bhagavad-gītā* that one who begins Kṛṣṇa consciousness cannot lose anything:

nehābhikrama-nāśo 'sti
pratyavāyo na vidyate
svalpam apy asya dharmasya
trāyate mahato bhayāt

"In this endeavor there is no loss or diminution, and a little advancement on this path can protect one from the most dangerous type of fear." (Bg. 2.40)

In the Sixth Chapter of *Bhagavad-gītā,* when Arjuna asks about the fate of the unsuccessful *yogī,* Śrī Kṛṣṇa replies:

pārtha naiveha nāmutra
vināśas tasya vidyate
na hi kalyāṇa-kṛt kaścid
durgatiṁ tāta gacchati

"Son of Pṛthā, a transcendentalist engaged in auspicious activities does not meet with destruction either in this world or in the spiritual world; one who does good, My friend, is never overcome by evil." (Bg.6.40)

The Lord then indicates that the unsuccessful *yogī* takes up his practice of Kṛṣṇa consciousness in the next life, beginning from the point where he left off. In other words, if one has finished fifty percent of the process in one life, in the next life he begins at fifty-one percent. Whatever material assets we accumulate in our life, however, are all annihilated at death, for we cannot take material opulence with us.

However, one should not think that he will do well to wait for the next life to attain Kṛṣṇa consciousness. We should try to fulfill the mission of Kṛṣṇa consciousness in this life. Kṛṣṇa promises us that one who becomes His devotee will come to Him without fail:

manmanā bhava mad-bhakto
mad-yājī māṁ namaskuru
mām evaiṣyasi satyaṁ te
pratijāne priyo 'si me

"Always think of Me. Become My devotee. Worship Me, and offer your homage unto Me. The result is that you will come to Me without fail. I promise you this, because you are My very dear friend." (Bg. 18.65)

When we think of coming to Kṛṣṇa, we should not think that we will be standing before a void or an impersonal bright light. Kṛṣṇa, God, is a person, just as we are persons. Materially we can understand that our father is a person, and that his father is also a person, and that his father's father is a person and so on back to the supreme father, who must also be a person. This is not very difficult to understand, and it is noteworthy that God is called the supreme father not only in the *Vedas* but in the Bible, Koran, and other scriptures. The *Vedānta-sūtra* also confirms that the Absolute Truth is the original father from whom everything has taken birth or emanated. This is also confirmed in the *Vedas:*

nityo nityānāṁ cetanaś cetanānām
eko bahūnāṁ yo vidadhāti kāmān

"The Lord is the supreme eternal amongst all eternals and the supreme living entity amongst all living entities. He is maintaining all others." The desires and life symptoms displayed by all living entities are simply reflections of the desires and life symptoms of the supreme father. In other words, our desires are born because He has desires. Because we are part and parcel of God, we have all the instincts of God in minute quantity. The sex play and sex life which we see in the material world is but the perverted reflection of the love that is found in the spiritual world. This world is material because God is forgotten here, but once He is remembered the world immediately becomes spiritual. In other words, the spiritual world is that place where Kṛṣṇa is not forgotten. That is also the definition of the spiritual world given by Vedic literatures. We must therefore plan our lives in such a way that it will not be possible for us to forget Kṛṣṇa for a moment. In this way, by engaging in the service of Kṛṣṇa, we will therefore always live in Vaikuṇṭha or Vṛndāvana, the abode of Kṛṣṇa.

At present, due to our polluted consciousness, we are turning the world into a materialistic and hellish place, and because we are ignorant of our constitutional position, we have created innumerable problems, just as in dreams we create so many problems. But in actuality there are no problems. I may dream that I am in a great storm, or that I am being pursued, or that someone is taking my money, or that I am being devoured by a tiger, but actually these are all creations of my mind. *Asaṅgo hy ayaṁ puruṣa iti śruteḥ.* The *Vedas* say that the *puruṣa* (the *ātmā* or the soul) has no connection with all its dreamlike material activities. Therefore we must engage in this Kṛṣṇa consciousness process to awaken from this dreaming condition.

Above all the fruitive laborers, speculators, and mystic *yogīs* are the *bhaktas,* or devotees of Kṛṣṇa. A *bhakta* can be perfectly peaceful, whereas the others cannot because everyone but the *bhakta,* one who has pure love, has desire. A *śuddha-bhakta* is desireless because he is simply happy serving Kṛṣṇa. He does not know or even care whether Kṛṣṇa is God or not; he just wants to love Kṛṣṇa. Nor is he concerned with the fact that Kṛṣṇa is omnipotent or that He is all-pervasive. In Vṛndāvana, the cowherd boys and the *gopīs* did not know whether Kṛṣṇa was God or not, but they simply loved Him. Although they were not Vedāntists, *yogīs* or *karmīs,* they were happy because they were simple village girls and boys who wanted to see Kṛṣṇa. This is a very highly elevated position called *sarvopādhi-vinirmuktaṁ tat-paratvena nirmalam,* or the stage of purity in which one is liberated from all material designations.

Although the *yogīs* and *jñānīs* are trying to understand God, they are not aware of their illusory condition. *Māyā-sukhāya bharam udvahato vimūḍhān:* They are fools because they are working hard for illusory happiness. There is no question of peace for them. The *jñānīs* or speculators, wanting to get relief from the hard work of this material world, reject this material world *(brahma satyaṁ jagan-mithyā).* Their position is a little higher than that of the *karmīs* because the *karmīs* have taken this material world as everything. They say, "Here we shall be happy," and their *dharma,* or religion, consists of trying to make a peaceful atmosphere within this material world. The fools do not know that this has been tried for millions of years but has never happened and never will happen. How can peace in the material world be possible when Kṛṣṇa, the creator Himself, says that this place is meant for trouble and miseries?

ābrahma-bhuvanāl lokāḥ
punar āvartino 'rjuna
mām upetya tu kaunteya
punar janma na vidyate

"From the highest planet in the material world down to the lowest, all are places of misery wherein repeated birth and death take place." (Bg. 8.16)

Duḥkhālayam aśāśvatam: not only is this world full of suffering, but it is also temporary. One cannot simply agree to go ahead suffering the three-fold miseries and stay here. Even that will not be allowed. In this world, he will not only be punished while staying here, but he will also be kicked out at the end. One may accumulate a large bank balance or an expensive home, a wife, children, and so many amenities, and he may think, "I am living very peacefully," but at any day he may be told, "Please get out."

"Why?" he will ask. "It is my house, and it is paid for. I have money and a job and responsibilities. Why should I get out?"

"Just get out. Don't talk. Get out."

On that day a man sees God. "Oh, I did not believe in God," he may think. "But now here is God finishing off everything." Thus it is said that the demoniac recognize Kṛṣṇa as death, for it is at that time that He takes everything away from them.

Why do we want to see God as death? When the demon Hiraṇyakaśipu saw Kṛṣṇa, he saw Him as death personified, but the devotee, Prahlāda, saw Him in His personal form as his beloved Lord. Those who challenge God will see Him in His ghastly aspect, but those who are devoted to Him will see Him in His personal form. In any case, everyone will ultimately see God.

A person who is honest can always see Kṛṣṇa everywhere. Kṛṣṇa says, "Try to understand Me. Try to see Me everywhere." By way of facilitating this method, the Lord says, *raso 'ham apsu kaunteya:* "I am the taste of water." When we are thirsty and need a glass of water, we can drink it and feel happy, understanding that the power of water to quench our thirst is Kṛṣṇa. Similarly, as soon as there is sunrise or moonshine, we can see Kṛṣṇa, for He says, *prabhāsmi śaśi-sūryayoḥ:* "I am the sun and moon." At a further stage we can see Kṛṣṇa as the life force within everything, as He indicates in *Bhagavad-gītā:*

puṇyo gandhaḥ pṛthivyāṁ ca
tejaś cāsmi vibhāvasau
jīvanaṁ sarva-bhūteṣu
tapaś cāsmi tapasviṣu

"I am the original fragrance of the earth, and I am the light in fire. I am the life of all that lives, and I am the penances of all ascetics." (Bg. 7.9)

Once we understand that all things are dependent upon Kṛṣṇa for their existence, there is no possibility of His ever becoming lost to us. In *Bhagavad-gītā* the Lord indicates that all things abide in Him in both their beginning and in their end and also in the interim state:

etad yonīni bhūtāni
sarvāṇīty upadhāraya
ahaṁ kṛtsnasya jagataḥ
prabhavaḥ pralayas tathā

mattaḥ parataraṁ nānyat
kiñcid asti dhanañjaya

mayi sarvam idaṁ protaṁ
sūtre maṇi-gaṇā iva

"Of all that is material and all that is spiritual in this world, know for certain that I am both its origin and dissolution. O conquerer of wealth (Arjuna), there is no truth superior to Me. Everything rests upon Me, as pearls on a thread." (Bg. 7.6,7)

Kṛṣṇa is easily visible, but He is only visible to those who are devoted to Him. For those who are envious, foolish or unintelligent, He obscures Himself with His veil of *māyā:*

nāhaṁ prakāśaḥ sarvasya
yoga-māyā-samāvṛtaḥ
mūḍho 'yaṁ nābhijānāti
loko māṁ ajam avyayam

"I am never manifest to the foolish and unintelligent. For them I am covered by My eternal creative potency *(māyā);* thus the deluded world knows Me not, who am unborn and infallible." (Bg. 7.25)

This eternal creative potency, or *yoga-māyā,* which obscures Kṛṣṇa to the unintelligent, is dissolved by love. This is the verdict of *Brahma-saṁhitā:*

premāñjana-cchurita-bhakti-vilocanena
santaḥ sadaiva hṛdayeṣu vilokayanti

"One who has developed love for Kṛṣṇa can see Him within his heart twenty-four hours a day."

Those who thus see Kṛṣṇa are not anxious because they know where they are going at death. One who has taken the gift of Kṛṣṇa consciousness knows that he will not have to return to this material world to take another body but that he will go to Kṛṣṇa. It is not possible to go to Kṛṣṇa unless one attains a body like Kṛṣṇa's, a *sac-cid-ānanda-vigraha* body, a body full of eternity, knowledge and bliss. One cannot enter into fire and not perish unless he himself becomes fire, and similarly one cannot enter into the spiritual realm in a body that is not spiritual. In a spiritual body one can dance with Kṛṣṇa in the *rāsa* dance like the *gopīs* and the cowherd boys. This is not an ordinary dance, but the dance of eternity, in the association of the Supreme Personality of Godhead. Only those who have become purified in their love for Kṛṣṇa can participate in it. One therefore should not take this process of Kṛṣṇa consciousness as something cheap, but as a matchless gift bestowed upon suffering humanity by the Lord Himself. Simply by engaging in this process, all the anxieties and fears of one's life, which in actuality revolve about the fear of death, are allayed.

APPENDIXES

GLOSSARY

Adhīra—one who is not sober and is always disturbed.
Adhokṣaja—not approachable or understandable by the material mind and senses; a name for Kṛṣṇa.
Ādi-puruṣa—Kṛṣṇa, the Supreme Primeval Person.
Ahaṁ brahmāsmi—"I am pure spirit soul."
Avidyā—ignorance, lack of knowledge.
Bhagavad-gītā—the scripture that records Lord Kṛṣṇa's eternal instructions to His friend Arjuna on the Battlefield of Kurukṣetra.
Bhaktas—devotees of Kṛṣṇa.
Bhakti-yoga—devotional service to the Supreme Lord.
Brahma-bhūtaḥ—the stage of liberation in which one realizes the Supreme Brahman and becomes free from hankering and lamentation.
Brahmacārī—a celibate student.
Brahmacarya—complete celibacy, the first principle of austerity.
Brahman—the all-pervading impersonal aspect of Kṛṣṇa.
Brāhmaṇa—a liberal, broad-minded person who knows the Absolute Truth.
Dhīra—one who is sober or undisturbed in spite of provocation.
Gopīs—the spiritual cowherd girl friends of Kṛṣṇa.
Gṛhasthas—Kṛṣṇa conscious householders.
Guru—spiritual master.
Jñāna—knowledge.
Jñāna-vairāgyam—that knowledge by which one becomes detached from material allurement.
Jñānīs—mental speculators.
Karma—any material action which will incur a subsequent reaction.

Karma-bandhanaḥ—work which binds one to this material world.
Karmī—one who works to enjoy the fruits of his labor.
Kevala bhakti—pure unalloyed devotional service in which there is no desire but to please Kṛṣṇa.
Kīrtanam—glorification of Kṛṣṇa.
Kṛpaṇa—a miserly man who does not use his human life for self-realization.
Kṛṣṇaloka—the eternal planet of Lord Kṛṣṇa in the spiritual sky.
Mahā-mantra—the great chanting for deliverance: Hare Kṛṣṇa, Hare Kṛṣṇa, Kṛṣṇa Kṛṣṇa, Hare Hare/ Hare Rāma, Hare Rāma, Rāma Rāma, Hare Hare.
Mahātmas—great souls.
Manu-saṁhitā—the Vedic lawbook for mankind.
Māyā—the illusory energy which causes the soul to forget God.
Mukti—liberation.
Paramparā—disciplic succession, the process of hearing from Kṛṣṇa or His representatives and repeating exactly what they have said.
Prasāda—spiritual food which has been offered to Kṛṣṇa.
Ṛṣis—great learned scholars and devotees.
Sac-cid-ānanda-vigraha—spiritual form full of eternity, knowledge and bliss.
Samādhi—trance, absorption in God consciousness.
Sannyāsa—the renounced order of life, free from family relationships.
Śāstras—revealed scriptures.
Smaraṇam—always remembering Kṛṣṇa.

Śravaṇam—hearing from an authorized source.
Śrīmad-Bhāgavatam—the Vedic scripture which specifically describes the pastimes of Lord Kṛṣṇa and His devotees.
Tapasvī—one who performs austerities.
Tapasya—austerity.
Tyāga—renunciation of the material world.
Vaikuṇṭhas—the eternal planets of the spiritual sky.
Vaiṣṇava—a devotee of the Supreme Lord, Kṛṣṇa.
Vāsudeva-parāyaṇāḥ—those who are devoted to Lord Kṛṣṇa (Vāsudeva).
Vimūḍhas—materialistic persons who have unnecessarily burdened themselves for temporary happiness.
Vṛndāvana—the site of Kṛṣṇa's pastimes when He appeared on earth 5,000 years ago.
Yajña—sacrifice, work done for Kṛṣṇa.
Yoga—the process of linking with the Supreme Lord.
Yogamāyā—the eternal creative potency of Kṛṣṇa which obscures Him to the unintelligent.

INDEX

ISKCON CENTERS AROUND THE WORLD

ISKCON is a worldwide community of devotees dedicated to the principles of *bhakti-yoga*. Write, call, or visit for further information. Classes are held in the evenings during the week, and a special feast and festival is held every Sunday afternoon.

AFRICA: **Durban, S. Africa**—c/o Popatlal Kara, 201 Grey St.; **Nairobi, Kenya**—P.O. Box 28946 (E. Africa)/ 31568.

ASIA: **Bombay, India**—Hare Krishna Land, Gandhi Gram Road, Juhu, Bombay 400 054/ 577315; **Calcutta, India**—3 Albert Road, Calcutta 700017/ 44-3757; **Hyderabad, India**—Hare Krishna Land, Nampally Station Road, AP; **Jakarta, Indonesia**—Gg. Kelinci IV: 8-A; **Kowloon, Hong Kong**—38 Mody Rd. 4/ fl., Tsim Sha Tsuy/ 3-668061; **Mayapur, India**—ISKCON International Center, PO Sree Mayapur Dham, W. Bengal (District Nadia); **New Delhi, India**—19 Todar Mal Lane, New Delhi 110001; **Taipei, Taiwan**—29-7, Hung Chow, South Rd., Section 2; **Tokyo, Japan**—Ichichome, 1-44 Mita, Minato-ku; **Vrindavana, India**—Krishna-Balarama Temple, Chattikara Road, Raman Reti, Mathura, UP/ 178.

AUSTRALIA: **Adelaide, Australia**—13A Frome St., S.A./ 020-253160; **Auckland, New Zealand**—67 Gribblehirst Rd., Mt. Albert/ 686-666; **Melbourne, Australia**—14 Burnett St., St. Kilda, Victoria 3182/ 663-1331; **Melbourne, Australia**—299 St. Lonsdale St., Victoria; **Sydney, Australia**—12 Wallaroy Crescent, Double Bay, NSW/ 365671.

EUROPE: **Amsterdam, Holland**—Herengracht 96/ 020-249410; **Berlin, W. Germany**—1 Berlin 31, Kurfurstendamm 153/ 8-86-25-39; **(Frankfurt A. Main), W. Germany**—6241 Schloss Rettershof, bei Konigstein-Taunus/ 06174-21357; **Geneva, Switzerland**—9, chemin du Credo, 1213 Petit Lancy/ 921-318; **Hamburg, W. Germany**—2 Hamburg 54, Kapitelbuschweg 20/ 570-53-82; **London, England**—7 Bury Place, Bloomsbury WC1/ 01-405-1463; **London, England**—Bhaktivedanta Manor, Letchmore Heath, Watford WD2 8EP, Hertfordshire/ Radlett, code 9276, 7244; **Manchester, England**—382 Great Clowes St., Salford 7, Lancs; **Munich, W. Germany**—8042 Oberschleissheim, Dr. Hoffmeister Str. 7/ 3150421; **Paris, France**—4 rue Le Sueur, 75016 Paris/ 727.02.02; **Rome, Italy**—Sede Centrale: Via Mistretta 2, (Piazza Lodi) 00182; **Stockholm, Sweden**—Solhagavagen 22, 16352 Spanga/ 760-0852.

LATIN AMERICA: **Buenos Aires, Argentina**—Ecuador 473; **Caracas, Venezuela**—Calle Luis Roche No. 61, Colinas, De Los Chaguaramos/ 76-74-57; **Mexico City, Mexico**—Gobernador Tiburcio, Montiel 45, San Miguel, Mexico City 18/ (905) 515-4242; **Rio Piedras, Puerto Rico**—55 Jorge Romany, Santa Rita, San Juan 90028/ (809) 764-1373; **Santa Domingo, Dominican Republic**—Calle Cayetano Rodriguez No. 36.

THE UNITED STATES AND CANADA: **Ann Arbor, Michigan**—718 W. Madison 48103/ (313) 665-6304; **Atlanta, Georgia**—24 N.E. 13th St. 30309/ (404) 892-9042; **Austin, Texas**—1003 E. 14th St. 78702/ (512) 476-1558; **Boston, Massachusetts**—72 Commonwealth Ave. 02116/ (617) 782-8892; **Boulder Creek, California**—257 Sylvan Way 95006/ (408) 338-4465; **Buffalo, New York**—132 Bidwell Pkwy. 14222/ (716) 882-0281; **Chicago, Illinois**—1014 Emerson St., Evanston 60201/ (312) 475-9126; **Cleveland, Ohio**—15720 Euclid Ave., E. Cleveland 44112/ (216) 851-9367; **Dallas, Texas**—5430 Gurley Ave. 75223/ (214) 827-6330; **Denver, Colorado**—1400 Cherry St. 80220/ (303) 333-5461; **Detroit, Michigan**—8311 E. Jefferson Ave. 48214/ (313) 824-6000; **Gainesville, Florida**—1800 N.W. 4th St., Apt. 34D 32601/ (904) 377-1496; **Honolulu, Hawaii**—1578 Ala Aoloa Loop 96819/ (808) 839-2210; **Houston, Texas**—107 Knox St. 77006/ (713) 869-7809; **Laguna Beach, California**—641 Ramona Ave. 92651/ (714) 494-9172; **Los Angeles, California**—3764 Watseka Ave. 90034/ (213) 871-0717; **Miami, Florida**—4001 Kumquat Ave., Coconut Grove 33133/ (305) 448-7893; **Montreal, Canada**—2051-53 Bleury Ave., Quebec/ (514) 849-4319; **New Orleans, Louisiana**—2936 Esplanade Ave. 70119/ (504) 448-1313; **New Vrindavana, West Virginia**—RD 1, Box 620, McCreary's Ridge, Moundsville, W. Virginia 26041/ (304) 845-2790; **New York, New York**—439 Henry St., Brooklyn 11231/ (212) 596-9658; **Ottowa, Canada**—224 Besserer St., Ontario/ (613) 236-9091; **Philadelphia, Pennsylvania**—424 E. Woodlawn St. 19144/ (215) 849-1767; **Pittsburgh, Pennsylvania**—4626 Forbes Ave. 15213/ (412) 683-7700; **Portland, Oregon**—2228 N.E. Union St. 97212/ (503) 284-6395; **Quebec City, Canada**—2377 Chemin St. Foy; **St. Louis, Missouri**—4544 Laclede Ave. 63108/ (314) 361-1224; **San Diego, California**—3303 Second Ave. 92103/ (714) 291-7778; **San Francisco, California**—455 Valencia St. 94103/ (415) 861-6464; **Seattle, Washington**—400 18th Ave. East 98102/ (206) 329-9348; **Toronto, Canada**—187 Gerrard St. East, Ontario M5A 2E5/ (416) 922-5415; **Vancouver, Canada**—1774 West 16th Ave., Vancouver-9, B.C./ (604) 732-8422; **Washington, D.C.**—2015 "Q" St. N.W. 20009/ (202) 667-3516; **Winnipeg, Canada**—160 Home St., Manitoba/ (204) 775-3575.